# AUTUMN WISDOM

# AUTUMN WISDOM

*A Book of Readings*

## RICHARD L. MORGAN

*Foreword by*
STEPHEN SAPP

UPPER
ROOM BOOKS
NASHVILLE

## Autumn Wisdom

Cover Design: Leigh Ann Dans
Cover Photograph: The Image Bank, Inc., Bullaty/Lomeo
Interior Design: Nancy Cole
First Printing: October 1995 (7)
Library of Congress Catalog Number: 95-60920
ISBN: 0-8358-0745-2

PRINTED IN THE UNITED STATES OF AMERICA

# Acknowledgments

*The publisher gratefully acknowledges permission to reprint the following copyrighted material:*

Laura Boone: "Death Is But a Horizon." Used by permission.

Frederick Buechner: From *Telling Secrets*. Copyright © 1991 by Frederick Buechner. Reprinted by permission of HarperCollins Publishers, Inc.

Donald X. Burt: From *But When You Are Older*. Copyright © 1992 by The Order of St. Benedict, Inc. Published by The Liturgical Press, Collegeville, MN. Used with permission.

John David Burton: "When Everybody Comes Back from the Cemetery Except Me" from *Naked in the Street*. Copyright © 1985 by John David Burton. Used by permission of the author.

George A. Buttrick: From *Prayer*. Copyright © 1952 by Whitmore & Stone. Used by permission of the publisher, Abingdon Press.

"Caregiver's Prayer" from *Prayers for Caregivers*. Ginter Park Presbyterian Church. Used by permission.

Mayme Carpenter: "Don't Call Me Old." Used by permission of the author.

Anthony De Mello: From *Heart of the Enlightened*. Copyright © 1989 by The Center for Spiritual Exchange. Used by permission of Doubleday, a division of Bantam Doubleday Dell Publishing Group.

Steven P. Eason: Reflections used by permission of the author.

Estelle Atley Eaton: "So Tired." Used by permission of the author.

Kenneth L. Gibble: From "Who Was Abishag?" Used by permission of the author.

Robert Giezentanner: "The Lost Tribes of Israel." Used by permission of the author.

Vivian E. Greenberg: From *Your Best Is Good Enough*. Copyright © 1989 by Lexington Books. Used by permission of Simon & Schuster, Inc.

Frank Hutchison: From *Aging Comes of Age*. Copyright © 1991 by Frank Hutchison. Westminster/John Knox Press, 1991.

Marshall Jenkins: From "Grandfather's Prayers." Copyright © 1993 by Christian Century Foundation. Reprinted by permission from the March 10, 1993 issue of *The Christian Century*.

Genevieve Lexow: "Come, Ye Elders, Those Engaging." Words copyright © 1976 by The Hymn Society, Texas Christian University, Fort Worth, TX 76129. All rights reserved. Used by permission.

Helen M. Luke: From *Old Age*. Reprinted by permission of the estate of Helen M. Luke.

Austin J. Lyman and Margie E. Edwards: "Elderly Hard Times" from *The Journal of Gerontological Social Work*, Vol. 14 (1/2) p. 86. Copyright © 1989 by The Haworth Press, Inc.

Mary McCorkle: Excerpts in "I've Enjoyed Every Minute of It." Used by permission.

*To the baby boomers in our family,*
*with the hope and conviction*
*that your aging will be bright and beautiful:*
*Rick, Cindy, Randy, Debbie,*
*Harding, Paige, Anna, and Dave.*

*No spring, nor summer beauty hath such grace,*
*As I have seen in one autumnal face.*

*John Donne, Elegy IX*

# Table of Contents

# Foreword

In the preface to this volume, Richard Morgan quotes the late Lutheran theologian Joseph Sittler's observation that a major shortcoming among contemporary gerontologists is their failure to hear what those whom they are studying—the increasing numbers of aging people in our country—have to say about the topic of aging. *Autumn Wisdom* is an admirable step in addressing this weakness.

Indeed, the strength of this book for me—as well as the real service Richard Morgan has rendered for all of us—is well expressed in the words of the Navajo Tom Ration in Meditation 14: "The stories that are told can be repeated . . . to make them last. If we keep them to ourselves, in about fifteen or twenty more years we will not have them." Most of the older people each of us knows may not have made the history books, but they have made the history—of our families, our churches, our communities, our nations. We must learn once again to listen to the stories of our elders because they are our history, our real history. If they are allowed to die with their stories untold (or unheard), then all of that history will die with them. The African proverb summarizes the situation well: "When a knowledgeable old person dies, a whole library disappears." Indeed, we have reached a time when we need to recall what simpler cultures have always known—that if we have to go where we have never been, it only makes sense to ask the way of those who are already there!

William F. May of Southern Methodist University is fond of telling a story about T.S. Eliot that is apropos here. After a lecture, a student asked, "But Mr. Eliot, what are we going to do about the problem you've just described?" Eliot replied that the student had asked the wrong question. "There are two kinds of problems we face in life," Eliot said. "One demands the question, 'What are we going to do about it?' and the other forces

us to ask, 'How are we to behave in the face of it?'"
Aging is clearly of the second type because at its most
fundamental level, there is nothing we can really do
about it. Each of us can and must, however, decide how
we are going to behave in the face of it.

As he has done so ably in *No Wrinkles on the Soul* and
*I Never Found That Rocking Chair*, so in this book Richard
Morgan—himself an excellent example of a positive and
healthy response to Eliot's question—gently leads the
reader into new insights and understanding of meaningful ways to behave in the face of the universal experience
of aging. Even more important, however, he helps us to
see—through the stories and words of those best suited
to offer useful answers, namely, those who have already
been there—that for Christians aging is an experience
we do not have to confront alone.

Stephen Sapp
Professor of Religious Studies
University of Miami
Coral Gables, Florida

# *Preface*

It has been five years since I wrote *No Wrinkles on the Soul*. I have been overwhelmed by the many responses from older persons and from those who care for elders. Many have shared precious stories of how they have used the book in various settings where older people live. I take heart in knowing that caregivers have read aloud from *No Wrinkles* to God's elderly saints who can no longer read. I find joy in hearing that some have used this book of meditations for devotional reading, either during the day or as last thoughts before drifting off to sleep at night. All this has made it worthwhile.

Yet, there seemed to be something missing, and I finally realized what it was. As I have traveled far and wide as an advocate for older persons, I have listened to their stories. I am convinced that much of their wisdom is being muted by our careless neglect. I have listened to the wisdom of many spiritual elders. I have sat by the wheelchairs of centenarians who tell stories of sorrow and joy from days gone by and have marveled at their incredible tales. Although it may be true that not all elderly become wise, these "wisdom people" have taught me that we desperately need the elders to keep us on course, to function as our mentors in this age.

I have sat where they sat, often in lonely homes, where they sit quietly by the windows, with haunting eyes searching for someone to come and spend time with them. With some reticence, I have spent hours with the frail elderly in nursing homes, holding their hands as they have grappled with issues of life and death. My journey has taken me into the homes and lives of many spiritual elders—mountain people with their fine lined faces, Native Americans, aged women past the century mark, and those whom I call "saints in wheelchairs."

One of the distressing features of many who describe aging is their lack of concern for the views of older people themselves. The voices of old people can tell us much about how it feels to be old. When they talk about themselves, they reveal a sense of self that Sharon R. Kaufman calls "the ageless self." It is my hope that through their stories, this "ageless self" will emerge from the pages of this book.

We live in both a grand and awful time to be growing older. The gift of bonus years has its blessings as well as its burdens. You who are caregivers of the elderly face challenges unknown to previous generations, as you experience your own aging, and yet try to meet the needs of older parents or relatives.

In Plato's *Dialogues*, Socrates talks about conversing with old men. He says, "I regard them as travelers who have gone on a journey on which I too may have to go, and of whom I ought to enquire, whether the way is smooth and easy, or rugged and difficult."

Listening to the autumn wisdom of these spiritual elders will convince us it is both—at times smooth, at other times rugged. But their deep spiritual wisdom will help make "the crooked places straight and the rough places smooth" for us.

My prayer is that you will listen to their wisdom, learn from their experience, and love their spirit as you grow older.

Let us all heed the wisdom of scripture: "Is not wisdom found among the aged? Does not long life bring understanding?" (Job 12:12).

Richard Morgan

# I

# A New Age Is Dawning

*With beauty before me may I walk,*
*With beauty behind me may I walk,*
*With beauty above me may I walk,*
*With beauty all around me may I walk.*
*In old age wandering on a trail of beauty,*
*Lively, may I walk.*

*Navajo Prayer*

# 1

For with you is the fountain of life; in your light we see light.

Psalm 36:9

## READ FOR REFLECTION

Each of us is nudged by the life-force within to become the person we are given the capacity to be—that self whose gradual process of becoming is his or her avenue into God, the Source, the Self from whence we come, in Whom we are invited to live our life with increasing fullness and freedom until God claims us totally.

EMMA LOU BENIGNUS

## *The Fountain of Age*

This *is* a new age of growing older. No longer are older persons seen as tottering, helpless, over-the-hill people, crotchety crones, and grumpy old men. With the conquest of premature death from disease, the extension of a healthy, vigorous life has become a realistic hope for most older people. Ponce de Leon's search for the fountain of youth, the waters of which had the power to restore youth, has finally ended. Betty Friedan's claim that people sixty and older are defining for themselves a good life that doesn't seek the fountain of youth, but instead affirms the fountain of age, is being confirmed every day.

Ironically, these bonus years mean we may well live into the long, late afternoon of life, and yet suffer from chronic illnesses before we die. No one can deny that people *are* living longer. Of all the people in the history of the world who have passed their sixtieth birthday, two-thirds are living today. But there is more here than longer life. There is an attitude shift. We are adopting a concept of aging as a new stage of life and growth.

Centuries ago the psalmist knew the secret to conscious aging regardless of how long a person lived. For him, the "fountain of life" was in God. God's unfailing love was priceless, and a living faith meant lifelong joy and an enduring sense that life has meaning.

 **PRAYER**

Living God, as we turn from our obsession with finding the fountain of youth to finding meaning in the fountain of age, let us not forget you, the fountain of life. Amen.

# 2

Do not remember the former things, Nor consider the things of old. Behold, I will do a new thing, Now it shall spring forth; Shall you not know it?

Isaiah 43:18, 19 (NKJV)

## READ FOR REFLECTION

There is a growing recognition today that life can have meaning and purpose for people in their later years. A wider world is opening up for those who were once considered permanently locked into a narrow existence.

It was discoverers like Columbus and Balboa and Cabot who opened new worlds to those living in Europe. In our day, older people are becoming joint discoverers. Men and women are embarking on a journey of exploration of life after retirement. They are pioneers in a new world where life at its best is not over when one's job ends or when the children leave home.

FRANK HUTCHISON

## MEDITATION

### *Three New Agers*

This week I visited three "new agers," all of whom were seventy-five or older. John had "retired" three times, and remained highly involved as a volunteer in mission with the church. His life witnessed to the truth of Charles Fahey's words, ". . . the Third Age . . . can be a time of conscious decision making, a graceful period in which older persons may return the gifts they have received, a time to reengage with the broader society." He told me, "My health is excellent. Why should I sit around? God's work goes on."

Susan had been active as a volunteer tutor for disadvantaged children, but she told me she was withdrawing from that so she could "wait on the Lord." It is in prayer that one can become more intentional and focused on how to use her or his gifts. "I am not allowing circumstances to dominate my time," she said, "but really trying to do God's will."

I spoke with Millie on her 102nd birthday, and she told me she was hard at work on her next book. The title? *I'm a Hundred and Two, and So Much to Do.* No idle sitting and passive life for her! Despite being in a wheelchair, her life was still full of unwritten books and unfinished symphonies.

These three model the "new agers," older people who are not senile, spent, or sessile. Vibrant and lively, they fulfill the words of the prophet. God *is* doing a new thing through them.

 PRAYER

Ancient of Days, you have no age. You continue to work through older persons whose spirit is ageless. Amen.

# 3

To the Jews who had believed him, Jesus said, "If you hold to my teaching, you are really my disciples. Then you will know the truth, and the truth will set you free."

John 8:31-32

## READ FOR REFLECTION

There is also a radical freedom from constraints and expectations of society, a "rolelessness" in later life that does not exist at earlier stages of the life span. While dreaded by most people and perceived by social scientists as a negative occurrence, I believe that this "radical freedom of age" has a spiritual purpose. Its acute discomfort can become the impetus that liberates adults to go beyond the ordinary, the usual, the expected, to birth love in new and creative and courageous ways and to publicly model the message of love.

JANE MARIE THIBAULT

## *This Radical New Freedom*

I have been blessed by older persons who daily demonstrate this radical new freedom of aging. Two persons come to mind.

An older woman who had devoted her life to others had always wanted to visit the Holy Land. Finances and work had always denied this dream, but after retirement she summoned her courage to become a tour guide at age seventy and now leads international tours to Israel. No doubt she had gone "beyond the ordinary, the usual, and the expected . . . in new and creative and courageous ways."

The second person, a postal worker, had to retire because of failing eyesight. He refused to feel sorry for himself. He found a "second career" in collecting over ten thousand hubcaps, and now has a successful business replacing those that have been stolen. Instead of raging at his aging, he found new directions for his latter years. As he told me, "Just because a person loses his eyesight, doesn't mean he can't have vision." His vision has meant a new freedom for his retirement years.

Jesus' words to the Jews who had believed in him lead us to a deeper understanding of freedom. Only as we are "truly his disciples," will we know the truth that sets us free. It is a freedom that comes from being loved by God and accepted despite our frailties and weaknesses.

 PRAYER

Compassionate God, help us to use our freedom for new beginnings. Amen.

Never again will there be in it an infant that lives but a few days, or an old man who does not live out his years; he who dies at a hundred will be thought a mere youth . . .

Isaiah 65:20

## READ FOR REFLECTION

Let these centenarians invite you to take a new look at old age, and in so doing, to take a new look at your own life, for they are what you are becoming with every passing day. They don't necessarily make old age look easy, but they do make it look worthwhile.

JIM HEYNEN

## MEDITATION

### I'm a Hundred Now, But Fine Anyhow

Mayme Carpenter was amazing. She began writing in her eighties because, "So many people kept asking me for copies of my poetry that it was easier to get them published than to make individual copies." At age ninety-nine, she wrote another book, entitled, *I'm 99 and Doing Fine!* One of her poems has been included in the *Congressional Record*.

When she became 100 years old, she was still working on her newest book, *I'm a Hundred Now, But Fine Anyhow.* What a commentary on her spirit. She traveled once by bus to a college reunion and when those who met her at the bus asked, "Did you come by yourself on the bus?" she replied, "Oh no. There were plenty of people on the bus with me!"

She began to accept the need to slow down when she reached ninety-eight and gave up driving. "I thought that I was too old to drive. I'd been driving since 1926 and always got a reduction for being a safe driver. I didn't want to spoil my record that late in the game," she said.

Moses was fortunate indeed to live to be 120, and "his eyes were not weak nor his strength gone" (Deut. 34:7). Other centenarians are not so fortunate, but like Mayme Carpenter, who lived to be 101, their resolute spirit amazes me. Mayme states in her poem "Don't Call Me Old":

> Don't call me old,
> But if you happen to forget
> The longer you live
> The more glorious seems the sunset.

**Let that be our Prayer for the day!**

# 5

READ GENESIS 5:25-27

Beloved, I pray that all may go well with you and that you may be in good health, just as it is well with your soul.

3 John 2 (NRSV)

## READ FOR REFLECTION

Grow old along with me!
The best is yet to be,
The last of life, for which the first was made:
. . . . . . . . . . . . . . . . . . . . . . . . . . . . . . . . . . . . . . .
But I need, now as then,
Thee, God, who mouldest men;
. . . . . . . . . . . . . . . . . . . . . . . . . . . . . . . . . . . . . . .
Amend what flaws may lurk,
What strain o' the stuff, what warpings past the aim!
My times be in Thy hand!
Perfect the cup as planned!

ROBERT BROWNING
(from "Rabbi Ben Ezra")

## MEDITATION

### *Methuselah Was Well-Preserved*

*(An imaginary conversation between Methuselah and his great-grandson, Shem.)*

*Methuselah:* Guess what I overheard someone at the campfire say about me last night? I heard him say, "You can say one thing for old Methuselah. He sure is well-preserved!" He really got my goat.

*Shem:* Well, you will celebrate your 969th birthday next month, and you *do* look old with that long, white beard. Even Grandfather can't remember you without it.

*Methuselah:* Well, I'd rather be called well-preserved, than badly preserved. But I still don't like that expression.

*Shem:* I know one thing, you sure have preserved your sense of humor and love of life. He can't call *you* a grumpy old man.

*Methuselah:* You know, Shem, that's the trouble with a lot of people. All they preserve is their grouchiness and constant complaining.

*Shem:* Yeah. Every time we play ball in old man Barsiluna's yard he yells at us and makes us leave.

*Methuselah:* Yes, Shem, even when our bodies grow old, there is something inside of us that can be preserved.

*Shem:* You mean, Great-grandpa, you can be younger than you look?

*Methuselah:* That's it. You know, I'm glad I am well-preserved.

 **PRAYER**

"Preserve me, O God, for in You I put my trust." Amen.
Psalm 16:1 (NKJV)

# 6

---

The righteous will flourish like a palm tree, they will grow like a cedar of Lebanon. . . . They will still bear fruit in old age, they will stay fresh and green.

Psalm 92:12, 14

---

## READ FOR REFLECTION

At evening,
I rest my arms awhile on the windowsill of Heaven,
And gaze upon the glory of God,
White fluffy clouds are floating across a bright
    blue sky.
In time, the sun slips down behind the mountains,
Leaving a golden glow. Soon colors begin to join
    the gold.
First faint, then brilliant—pink, mauve, lilac, and blue.
The majestic mountains reach up to absorb the muted
    tones.
After a while the colors slowly fade, leaving an
    afterglow.
A new moon appears high in the sky.
It is twilight.
Who but God could create such moving beauty!

ELIZABETH WALKER
("Evening at Grace Ridge," written at age 94)

## *Late Bloomers*

Tyrone Burkette tells about a particular tree on the campus of Livingstone College in North Carolina. During spring all the other trees would hastily bud and bring forth flowers and leaves, but this particular tree always had a late start in blooming. Some questioned whether the tree should be discarded, and cut down as hopeless and even dead. However, the president, the late Dr. Samuel E. Duncan, would say, "This tree is a late bloomer. Always behind, but it is sure to bloom."

Like the tree, late bloomers are always in our midst, especially in the ranks of older persons. Michelangelo was still designing churches at eighty-eight. Benjamin Franklin helped to write the Constitution when he was eighty-one. And the late bloomer par excellence was Grandma Moses, who began painting at age seventy-five, because, as she said, she was "too old to work on the farm and too young to sit on the porch." Nor is creativity in later life limited to a few people of exceptional artistic or scientific talent. Countless numbers of older persons have summoned their own personal resources and discovered that their most creative moments have been in the winter of life.

Surely we can make a case that Moses, Abraham, and Sarah were late bloomers, whose major roles in the salvation history did not begin until late in life. Late bloomers are an inspiration to those who live longer, and can still be green and fresh!

 PRAYER

Lord of our later years, may we bloom where we have been planted, right at the end of the row! Amen.

# 7

Consider the rock from which you were hewn, the quarry from which you were dug. Consider Abraham your father and Sarah who gave you birth.

Isaiah 51:1-2 (NJB)

## READ FOR REFLECTION

Even though you may feel overwhelmed, too old, or perhaps not quite ready to respond to this spiritual invitation to conscious awareness of your oneness with God, be confident that you really have been well-prepared to receive this gift. Each day of your life has prepared you for this vocation. This is the first time in the history of humankind that there are so many people over the age of sixty-five. Why? At this stage in the history of humankind you are called to be another Abraham, a new Sarah. The world, which is so afraid of the aging process, needs you to model—define, demonstrate, and preach— the meaningfulness of later life. It has never been done before. You are to be prophet in this time.

JANE MARIE THIBAULT

## MEDITATION

### *Called to Be a New Sarah*

Margaret reminds me of a new Sarah. Born during the early 1920s in the rural south, where her mother ironed and washed for others to make ends meet, she endured many hard knocks. She had to overcome the trauma of being a battered spouse, and the embarrassment of explaining blackened eyes and bruises to her friends. Later in life she suffered major tragedies in the senseless murders of her daughter, killed by an intruder, and her grandson, slain as an innocent bystander in a moment of violence.

She told me, "I gave my life to Christ when I was thirteen, and that has made all the difference." She has lived out the counsel of her father who told her, "The sky's the limit . . . stand tall and be all that you can be." She has been a tower of strength in the community, church, and neighborhood.

But, like Sarah, God now calls Margaret into a new vocation in her later years. Although her days and nights are full with caregiving for her husband, she has become a role model for younger women with her active involvement in the life of the community and church.

Her faith is genuine. She told me, "I asked the Lord to take care of me so I can live a full and active life, and He has answered that prayer. But I tell my children, 'Don't worry about me when I do get old. I'll just sign myself in at the nursing home and help other old folks!'"

 PRAYER

Gracious God, help us to make each day a new adventure in faith. Amen.

Nicodemus said to Him, "How can a man be born when he is old? Can he enter a second time into his mother's womb and be born?"

John 3:4 (NKJV)

## READ FOR REFLECTION

> I do not know if I am old
> I've had no such direction,
> The stages that I've heard about
> Somehow defy detection.
>
> I wonder, when all is said and done,
> If inventors of the stages
> Are using, in their research schemes,
> Some books with missing pages.
>
> Is it ego-integrity or despair?
> Or, did I leave stage seven?
> The only threshold I affirm
> Is the one that leads to heaven.
>
> Today I'm who I was before,
> The same tomorrow I will be;
> I'm reinforced by who I am
> Within a named community.
>
> I find that every "stage" of life
> Is part of *all* my days,
> A gift of that which makes me whole
> And gives me cause for praise.

WESLEY F. STEVENS
("On Not Growing Old by Stages")

## *The Ageless Self*

When asked if he was "born again," one elderly gentleman responded, "No, I was born right the first time." In a sense he was right. Aging means that we must find ways to be faithful to this "ageless self" we have been all our lives.

Two examples of this come to mind. A retired professor in a retirement community had always been a man of compassion. Now he visits daily the Health Care Center where he holds the hand of his comatose wife. She hasn't known him for years, but he comes and sits and whispers, "I love you . . ."

Another example is an artist who died recently in his late eighties. He had always been a person of great creativity and ingenuity. When he found he could no longer hold a brush in his right hand, he switched to his left!

We bring to old age the person we have become all our lives, and that means moments of being born again can repeatedly occur. Nicodemus was startled when Jesus confronted him with being "born again," especially at his old age. Yet Jesus was saying to him that conversion is a lifelong process and every age brings opportunities for new birth. New life and joy can be experienced at any stage of life, and especially so in our later years.

 PRAYER

O Creative Spirit, who has nurtured us all our lives with new births, make us even more vulnerable now to being born from above. Amen.

# 9

---

I wait for the LORD, my soul waits, and in His word I do hope.

Psalm 130:5 (NKJV)

Those who wait on the LORD shall renew *their* strength.

Isaiah 40:31 (NKJV)

---

## READ FOR REFLECTION

If and when the day comes that you are no longer active, look to the example of Simeon and Anna in the story of Jesus' Presentation in the Temple. Simeon was a just and pious man waiting to see the Messiah. Anna was a widow constantly in the temple worshiping. She talked about the Messiah to all she encountered. The Holy Spirit revealed to Simeon and Anna that they would not experience death until they had seen Jesus, the Messiah.

They set a fine example as older persons waiting for Jesus' coming into their own hearts and into the hearts of humanity. Maybe you, too, could ask God that you not experience death until you have seen Jesus closely in your own thoughts and in the faces of the people you serve.

LEO E. MISSINNE

## MEDITATION

### *Waiting with Hope*

Elizabeth, a widow, is a good example of an older person who waits for the coming of the Lord. Her devotion to God is evident in her service to humankind. She visits people in nursing homes, takes them to the doctor, and brings gifts of encouragement and love. Elizabeth never allowed herself the luxury of prolonged grief over her husband's death, but poured out her life in selfless service to others, especially older people in nursing homes.

Like Anna, Elizabeth was constantly in the church, worshiping. She was always the first there on Sunday morning, attending to the bulletins, checking the furnace, and preparing God's house for worship. Like Anna, she was always there offering hope and care to others. Elizabeth was able to be a source of strength to so many because her hope was in the Lord. This hope provided her renewed strength.

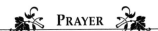 **PRAYER**

Thank you, gracious God, for choosing what is weak in the world to shame the strong! Amen.

# II

# Spiritual Elders: Through Aging Eyes

*To enter the country of age is a new experience, different from what you supposed it to be. Nobody, man or woman, knows the country until he has lived in it and has taken out his citizenship papers.*

*Malcolm Cowley*

# 10

Your beauty should not come from outward adornment . . . . Instead, it should be that of your inner self, the unfading beauty of a gentle and quiet spirit, which is of great worth in God's sight.

1 Peter 3: 3-4

## READ FOR REFLECTION

Those who are ignorant or neglectful of their spiritual well-being rarely enjoy a serene and fulfilled life.

FRANK HUTCHISON

## *The Raccoon Lady*

She is remarkable for her age. In her eightieth year, she was going strong, working in her garden, busy in her church work. Once we had a work day at the church and cleaned out the basement, and she outworked us all. When a stranger stopped and watched us, he seemed upset to see the work being done by older people, and asked, "Where are all the young people? They should be doing this work!" Mary Alice replied, "*We* are the young people of this church."

Even adversity evoked a touch of humor from this ageless lady. One day after church she lost control of her car and drove into a tree. She was not seriously hurt, but suffered bruises and blackened eyes. She called herself "the raccoon lady," because of those blackened eyes!

Mary Alice is one of our best teachers on growing older, for she shows us how to resist a tendency to become self-preoccupied as she reaches out to embrace others and the world. She has a spiritual inner beauty which is a revelation, an "unfading beauty of a gentle and quiet spirit" (1 Pet. 3:4).

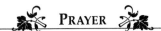 **PRAYER**

Lord, let us learn from older people the ability to find humor in adversity and joy in everyday life. Amen.

But God chose what is foolish in the world to shame the wise; God chose what is weak in the world to shame the strong.

1 Corinthians 1:27 (NRSV)

## READ FOR REFLECTION

The limits that come with age can be a peaceful release. New ventures are precluded by lack of time and energy. Others have ceased to have grandiose expectations of us. We are no longer their "problem solver." . . . No one expects us to run a marathon or start a new career or have a new family. We can walk now and need not run. We have become whatever we at an earlier time could come to be. . . .

Now we sing the final stanza of the song that is our life— a providential rhythm which dictates that each of us enters the course of time quietly, gradually grows in strength, makes our mark, and then sits back and watches a new age take over the reins of power. In these last quiet days the time for delusions of grandeur are over. If people are to love us now, they must love us for what we *are* for them rather than for what we can *do* for them.

Our souls are stilled and quiet, finally weaned from the passion to be more than we are, from the pretense of being more than we could ever be. We sit still in the embrace of God's providence, like a weaned child on its mother's lap.

DONALD X. BURT

## MEDITATION

### *Just a Little Pickup*

I first met Wanda at a symposium on aging and was admittedly curious when they wheeled this 102-year-old wonder into the assembly hall to speak to us. In a matter of minutes I became her captive, held spellbound by her brilliant mind, radiant spirit, and ageless beauty.

In a creaky voice, hardly above a whisper, she gave us the gift of her harvested wisdom. Commenting on the fact that she was one of 35,000 centenarians in the country, she said, "I don't know whether I am a centipede or a centurion! When people tell me to 'keep on trucking' I like to reply, 'I no longer drive a four-wheeler, only a little pickup!' But what a pickup!"

Wanda lives alone in an old house and is tough as nails. She has not only survived, but thrived by her belief in God's presence in her life. She is a wonderful model of a woman aging gracefully, moving toward the light, toward the ultimate source of all. And I am sure that there are many Wandas, from whom we learn the meaning of life.

Paul told the Corinthians that God had chosen what is weak to shame the strong. It may well be that we will learn what it means to have an unshakable faith in the love of God from people like Wanda, weakened by the years, but strong in faith.

 **PRAYER**

Grant us, O God, a faith that does not shrink. Amen.

# 12

I appeal to you for my son Onesimus, who became my son while I was in chains. Formerly he was useless to you, but now he has become useful both to you and to me.

Philemon 10-11

## READ FOR REFLECTION

We are not "senior citizens" or "golden-agers." We are the elders, the experienced ones; we are maturing, growing adults responsible for the survival of our society. We are not wrinkled babies, succumbing to trivial, purposeless waste of our years and our time.

MAGGIE KUHN

## MEDITATION

### *Useful Once More*

Howard was very old and tired. He had battled cancer for some time and constantly worried about his frail wife. He told me that at times he felt discarded, like an old car on a junk heap. When I asked him to play Santa Claus at a nursing home, he agreed reluctantly.

When Santa arrived that night, the people sat in wheelchairs and gerichairs, lined up in the halls. When they saw Santa, they yanked at his white beard, laughed at his husky ho-ho-hos, and sang carols with him. Soon he was gone, leaving a trail of good will and joy that would linger for a long time.

Howard felt useful once more. For one brief moment, despite his age, he felt valued and appreciated again. He knew hard days were ahead, as the ravages of age would continue their conquest. But on that night he was reborn, needed by others, no longer useless.

Onesimus was a runaway slave whom Paul befriended. Formerly he had been useless, but befriended by Paul, he had become useful. Now Paul urges Philemon to accept him back as a dear brother.

We can find countless stories today of older people who need the encouragement Paul gave Onesimus. Discarded by a productive society, they yearn to be needed and useful once more.

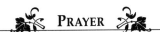 PRAYER

Healer of Persons, help all who feel discounted and useless to find someone who encourages them and restores their self-esteem. Amen.

# 13

Although Daniel knew that the document had been signed, he continued to go to his house, which had windows in its upper room open toward Jerusalem, and to get down on his knees three times a day to pray to his God and praise him.

Daniel 6:10 (NRSV)

## READ FOR REFLECTION

In a kindling book about prayer, E. Herman has reminded us of the story of "The Nun of Lyons." She was dancing at a fashionable ball. None was gayer or lovelier: her marriage to the most eligible man of her set was due within a week. Suddenly, in the midst of a minuet, she saw the vision of the world dying—for lack of prayer. She could almost hear the world's gasping, as a drowning man gasps for air. The dance now seemed macabre, a dance of death. In the corner a priest, smiling and satisfied, discussed the eligibles with a match-making mother: even the Church did not know the world was dying—for want of prayer. As instant as a leaping altar flame, she vowed her life to ceaseless inter-cession, and none could dissuade her. She founded a contemplative order of prayer—lest the world should die. Was she quite wrong? Was she wrong at all? Or is our world saved by those who keep the windows open on another World?

GEORGE A. BUTTRICK

## MEDITATION

### *Raising the Drawbridge at Sunset*

In ancient castles the custom of lifting the drawbridge at sunset signaled the closing out of the busy world and its distractions and settling down to the quiet and rest of the night. The bridge over the moat which surrounded every castle could be lowered in any hour of danger, but the sunset hour meant the day and its duties were over, and quiet rest of the night was assured.

Daniel, an exiled Jew, also had a drawbridge that he lifted to enter into quiet and rest. It was prayer. He prayed morning, noon, and night through open windows to Jerusalem. His strength and courage under fire came from "keeping the windows of his soul open on another World."

Older people tell me that prayer becomes a way they can "be" with loved ones, even though absent. Prayer helps them to go where they couldn't go. The draw-bridge is raised as the sunset years descend, and it becomes a time for quiet prayer and meditation for others and for the lost world.

 PRAYER

Pray these words of Sabine Baring-Gould's hymn for yourself and other older people facing the sunset of life:

Now the day is over, Night is drawing nigh,
Shadows of the evening Steal across the sky.
Jesus, give the weary Calm and sweet repose;
With Thy tenderest blessing May mine eyelids close.
Comfort every sufferer Watching late in pain;
Those who plan some evil From their sin restrain.
When the morning wakens, Then may I arise
Pure, and fresh, and sinless In Thy holy eyes. Amen.

# 14

For whatever is born of God overcomes the world. And this is the victory that has overcome the world—our faith.

1 John 5:4 (NKJV)

## READ FOR REFLECTION

I have survived in the past.
I can do it again now.
I've gotten over things before.
I can do it again.

I've faced bad weather, bears, wolves and white men.
I can also face old age.
No matter how bad things were I still went out
    with the sheep.
I will still go on regardless of my age.

We accept things as they are,
Not as hardships but as reality.
It is the same with old age.
We accept it.
. . . . . . . . . . . . . . . . . . .
I am not giving up now.
I never gave up in the past.
I am not giving up.
I have never given up.

AUSTIN J. LYMAN AND MARGIE E. EDWARDS
("Elderly Hard Times")

## *I Survived the White Man*

Driver Pheasant, a Native American from the Cherokee tribe, had lived on the reservation all his life. He recalled older days, when older American Indian people were the keepers and protectors of the tribal values and traditions. He remembered Swimmer, the greatest of Cherokee storytellers. He recalled how Swimmer kept the fire where the aging myth-keepers and priests sat in circles and told their stories.

He remembered the days when it was not unusual for children, youth, and young adults to address older American Indian people as "grandmother" or "grandfather," regardless of blood ties to the older person. "But now that is no longer true," he said with a sigh. "Our older ones now go to the Senior Center and play games . . . no one really takes the time to listen to them anymore. Yes, we have suffered in the past, but now we suffer from neglect." As I left him, I recalled the words attributed to Tom Ration, a Navajo:

> The stories that are told can be repeated . . .
> to make them last. If we keep them to
> ourselves, in about fifteen or twenty more years
> we will not have them. It will all be gone.
> There will not be any songs or prayers
> because the legends go along with all this.
> One cannot exist without the other.

 **PRAYER OF BLACK ELK**

Great Spirit, Great Spirit, my Grandfather, all over the earth the faces of living things are all alike. . . . Look upon these faces of children without number and with children in their arms, that they may face the winds and walk the good road to the day of quiet. Amen.

# 15

To him who can keep you from falling and bring you safe to his glorious presence, innocent and joyful, to the only God, our Saviour, through Jesus Christ our Lord, be glory, majesty, authority, and power, before all ages, now and for ever. Amen

Jude 24 (NJB)

## READ FOR REFLECTION

Soon-a will be done-a with the troubles of the world,
Troubles of the world, The troubles of the world.
Soon-a will be done-a with the troubles of the world.
Goin' home to live with God.
No more weeping and a-wailing,
No more weeping and a-wailing.
No more weeping and a-wailing,
I'm goin' to live with God.

(Traditional African American Spiritual)

## MEDITATION

### *Lord, Prop Me Up on Every Leaning Side!*

John has not had an easy life. Comparing his life to a river, there have been some moments of calm water, but mostly seasons of turbulent rapids and rocky boulders. Born into a poor African American family in the rural south, John knew the endless struggles of minority people.

Yet his contagious optimism overcame those barriers, and he has lived an admirable life in the community. Later in life, he faced the unspeakable tragedy of the suicide of one of his sons, and his own battle with cancer. But his philosophy has always been, "If I hold up, the Lord will show up," and that tells the story of his faith.

When he retired, he found a new vocation in managing the clothes closet at the Yokefellow Christian Center in the community. He told me that the words of Jesus were like thunderbolts in his soul: "When did we see you a stranger . . . lacking clothes and clothe you?" (Matt. 25:38, NJB). Countless numbers of poor and needy have found in John a person who not only clothes their bodies, but warms their souls.

On one occasion he told me that his constant prayer was, "Lord, prop me up on every leaning side." John has known more than his share of leaning sides in his lifetime. But he is a shining witness of how the Lord has propped him up.

 PRAYER

God of grace and God of glory, how often we fall under the pressures of life. Prop us up on every leaning side. Amen.

49

# 16

As Peter entered the house, Cornelius met him and fell at his feet in reverence. But Peter made him get up. "Stand up," he said, "I am only a man myself."

Acts 10:25-26

## READ FOR REFLECTION

When he was twenty, the writer Mark Twain said he was saddened to find his father out of touch with the times. And when he turned twenty-one, he was amazed to discover how much his father had learned in one year. . . .

My father was a minister in Philadelphia. He joked that our ancestors were either pastors or horse thieves—and he wasn't sure of the difference. He had the rare gift of laughing at himself.

After having served churches in Indiana, Kentucky, and Philadelphia, he retired at age seventy, but continued to preach. His last sermon, preached three days before his death, dealt with finding joy in life, in making each day worth living. . . .

The last time I saw him he talked about his death and gave gifts to his granddaughter.

The death of a parent, Freud said, is one of the most traumatic experiences of life; the loss leaves a void which nothing can fill. . . .

In the future, our parents will live longer. Rather than becoming burdens on us, they should become reflections of our own future and mentors to learn about living.

JOHN C. MORGAN

## *Don't Call Me a Senior Citizen!*

When my father grew older, he talked about himself as "the patriarch," and "the old man," but he never wanted to be called a "senior citizen." He never went to a senior center, and often seemed uneasy about taking Social Security checks. He lived all his life in a manse, and never owned his own home.

For over fifty-five years he was a pastor and had a special ministry to the aged in his church and community. He literally tramped hundreds of miles across the city visiting the aged, bringing them the sacrament, and conducting worship in homes for the aged. On many occasions he sat by the bedsides of the dying, holding their hand as their spirit passed into the next world.

His life reminds me of the story of Peter and Cornelius, when the centurion got down on his knees in worship of Peter. "Stand up; I am only a man myself," Peter declared. He had no desire to be worshiped or to receive the devotion of others. Peter only wanted to point beyond himself to the Lord whom all should worship.

Howard Moody Morgan was such a person. One of the treasured family stories is when his youngest son, John, was once asked by a church member if he was going to be a preacher like all the rest of the family, and his reply was, "Nope! I'm going to work!" This servant of God worked hard all his life to make a bridge between his humanity and other people. He may never have wanted the title, "Senior Citizen," but he helped many older persons become citizens of that city with foundations.

 PRAYER

Loving Father, we know too well our humanity and weakness as we grow older. Help us to use our weakness to make others strong. Amen.

# 17

Many women have done admirable things, but you surpass them all! Charm is deceitful, and beauty empty; but the woman who fears Yahweh is the one to praise.

Proverbs 31:29, 30 (NJB)

## READ FOR REFLECTION

She excoriated the ravages of old age but never accepted them as the inevitable consequences of getting old. "I don't know what's wrong with me today," she must have said a thousand times as she tried once, then again, then a third time, to pull herself out of her chair into her walker. It never seemed to occur to her that what was wrong with her was that she was on her way to pushing a hundred. Maybe that was why some part of her remained unravaged. Some surviving lightness of touch let her stand back from the wreckage and see that among other things it was absurdly funny. When I told her the last time she was mobile enough to visit us in Vermont that the man who had just passed her window was the gardener, she said, "Tell him to come in and take a look at the last rose of summer."

FREDERICK BUECHNER

## MEDITATION

### *The Last Rose of Summer*

She lives in a deteriorating house on a deserted dirt road in the hills of western North Carolina. Since her husband's death she has lived alone and is stranded except for those who take her to the store and the doctor. She is one of many rural older persons who remain out of sight, if not out of mind.

She told me that it is "mighty lonely" at times, but she talks with the Lord every day, and so far, "He has carried me through." Her living room seemed cluttered with old photos and memorabilia from her past, and she seemed eager to tell me her life story.

"You see," she said, "My family doesn't seem that interested in these memories. They're all so busy with their own lives," she added, with no bitterness or rancor in her voice. "I do feel like the last leaf on a tree, hanging by a thread. But I don't complain. God has been good to me."

As I left her presence with a prayer, I noticed these words on a plaque near the door, "As for me and my house, we will serve the LORD." She was "a last rose of summer," but her spirit reminded me of Isaiah's prophecy that "the desert shall rejoice and blossom like the rose" (Isa. 35:1, NKJV). In this humble place a woman of faith lived.

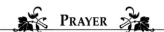 **PRAYER**

Remember with us tonight, O God, the old and help-less—those who have reached length of days and known life with its joys and bitterness and have come in the evening to the long shadows, unloved and uncared for and alone. Amen.

A Prayer of W.E.B. Du Bois

## 18

He shall be like a tree planted by the rivers of water, that brings forth its fruit in its season.

Psalm 1:3 (NKJV)

A word aptly spoken is like apples of gold in settings of silver.

Proverbs 25:11

## READ FOR REFLECTION

Only the elderly can appreciate the message of a sturdy tree that remains itself through every season and every condition of its life.

MARIA REILLY

### Clyde, the Apple Man

Clyde still sells apples while sitting on a lonely seat in a deserted church parking lot.

I stop to talk and buy apples. He talks, glad that someone listens.

He tells me his favorite song is "Just a Little Talk with Jesus Makes It Right," his eyes dim with tears.

I wonder why. What memories lurk behind those misty eyes, what pain?

"When you are ninety years old, you know some answers, but no one asks you any questions," he says. And adds, "My favorite Bible verse is in the Psalms, 'Be still, and know that I am God.'"

"Yes," I answer, "That's in Psalm 46."

I know Psalm 46. He knows God. I walk away and wonder . . . Is there really any difference between us?

Two older men, suspended in time, trying to eke out some meaning as life winds down. The Apple Man and the Preacher.

 **PRAYER**

Our Refuge and Strength, we would be still and know that you are our God. Amen.

# 19

I have learned to be content whatever the circumstances. I know what it is to be in need, and I know what it is to have plenty. I have learned the secret of being content in any and every situation . . .

Philippians 4:11-12

## READ FOR REFLECTION

For a "good old age," of course, freedom is a prerequisite, right in line with our current emphasis on independence, the individual, and the value of autonomy. True freedom, however, comes from security, and this suggests that some other values are also important because security, especially in old age when one's own powers and abilities inevitably decline, depends on others and their willingness to assist. If all of us could recapture a lively sense of our ultimate and absolute dependence, a large step would be taken toward a renewed recognition of our need for one another and thus our necessary *interdependence*. . . . This shift in attitude might make the increased dependence upon other people that accompanies growing older easier to accept.

STEPHEN SAPP

## *She Ages in Place*

Mildred has learned how to age in place. Now in her 101st year, she still lives in a wood-frame house, where sheets of plastic line the three sides of her back porch on which a Christmas cactus blooms. Inside, she sits in a wooden rocker in front of an old upright piano.

She smiled as she looked at the tattered pages of an old song from 1910. "You know, things have really changed for old folks since that song was written." I walked over and read the lines from its timeworn pages:

> "They say we are aged and grey, Maggie,
> As spray by the white breakers flung,
> But to me you're as fair as you were, Maggie,
> When you and I were young.
> And now we are aged and grey, Maggie,
> And the trials of life nearly done,
> Let us sing of the days that are gone, Maggie,
> When you and I were young."

"Shucks," she said, "That song is a curiosity. Why, today we don't pine for the good old days, we just live now. I know I have to rely on my neighbors, but I'm still hoeing to the end of the row."

There was something about the indomitable spirit of this little old woman that helped me realize she had learned the lesson of interdependence. She had acknowledged her total dependence on God, and could rely on others for help. She had learned "to be content whatever the situation!"

 PRAYER

We commit to your care, O Lord, all those who are full of years. Grant that as they suffer so many losses, they may not lose you. Give them light at evening, and the strength of interdependence. Amen.

# 20

The widow who is really in need and left all alone puts her hope in God and continues night and day to pray and to ask God for help.

1 Timothy 5:5

## READ FOR REFLECTION

We have to accept that learning to pray in later life is a different thing from learning early in life. I have the impression that Christians who have enjoyed long years of church membership learn the lessons of prayer in a gradual, natural way, almost imperceptibly integrating a lifetime of experiences into their prayers. But after we retire, time is short in which to learn the greatest thing in life—to search for God and to try to know him and to love him. Many great saints who have given up a whole lifetime to prayer have said that even after fifty years they were still beginners in prayer. But that need not deter us, even though we are well into our seventies or eighties.

SUSAN COUPLAND

## MEDITATION

### *We Have to Help the Lord Answer Our Prayers*

I never went to see her in the nursing home without her asking that we "unite in prayer" for other people. She was now ninety-seven years young, and though the years had broken her body, her spirit was full of life.

She hadn't been able to be in church in years, and her arthritic hands limited her ability to hold a Bible. She was almost blind, so she could not see the scriptures or read her books. But she could pray.

Ora's prayer life made me realize that prayer is really prayerfulness, the art of centering oneself, of being attentive. And prayerfulness is spirituality made concrete. Listening to this saintly lady pray for others made me believe that I understand what Jesus meant when he said, "Ask and it will be given to you; seek and you will find; knock and the door will be opened to you" (Matt. 7:7).

Sometimes we are so brash as to think that our visits to the frail elderly in nursing homes bring the gospel. I assure you that I never left the presence of this wizened saint without receiving the gospel from her. Her hope is in God, a constant reminder of the words of the psalm, "Whom have I in heaven but you? And there is nothing on earth that I desire other than you" (Psalm 73:25, NRSV).

 PRAYER

Lord of Prayer, we ask, "Teach us to pray." Among the ways we find that answer is in the prayers of older people. Amen.

# III

# Grace for the Creaky Days

*Older adulthood brings to almost everyone an increased body awareness and some physical deterioration if not a major assault upon the body. . . . We cannot hide these experiences from ourselves. We cannot deny them.*

*Roy W. Fairchild*

Remember your Creator while you are still young,
before the bad days come, before the years come which,
you will say, give you no pleasure.

Ecclesiastes 12:1 (NJB)

## READ FOR REFLECTION

Then come the creaky days.
The years creep up in which one feels
Like saying I have no taste for them.
Dimmed is the light of the moon
And the stars and the vision is patchy
Like a cloudy sky after the rain.
The hands and the arms, the guardians of the house
Begin to tremble, and the legs
Like battle-tired soldiers
Are unsure in their step.
The grinding mills, the teeth are fewer,
And the windows of the mind fog up.
The lips, the doors that open to the marketplace
Want to stay closed, and sounds heard get duller.
One's sleep is shallow and easily disturbed
By the twittering of a bird.
The gates of song are clogged
The back is bent
And the urge to mate is weakened
As a person walks to his eternal home.

TRANSLATION BY RABBI ZALMAN SCHACHTER-SHALOMI

## MEDITATION

### *Before the Creaky Days Come*

We may resist the pessimistic mood of the writer of the book of Ecclesiastes, but no one can deny the reality of what he writes. Koheleth, the Hebrew title of the author of this book, warns his readers to "remember their Creator in the days of their youth before the creaky days come," and then describes the frailties of old age in vivid language. For the writer, the shadow of decline and death hangs over the powerful as well as the oppressed.

While we applaud all the marvels of modern medicine that make aging easier, no one can deny the inevitable losses and debilities that come. The ancient writer of Ecclesiastes well understands what happens as our bodies age, as we move ever closer to our eternal home.

When Groucho Marx and Will Rogers traveled the vaudeville circuit, they often had baseball teams which they pitted against each other during their off afternoons. One afternoon Groucho's team was playing Rogers and his team. Groucho, who was on first base, was forced to run to second when the batter hit what should have been a sure double-play ball. But when the shortstop threw the ball to Rogers, who was ten years older than Groucho, he was standing twenty feet from the bag.

Groucho reached second safely standing up, but Rogers insisted that he was out! "What are you talking about?" complained Groucho. "You were nowhere near second base when you caught the ball." Rogers replied, "Groucho, when you get to be my age, any place you stand is second base."

 **PRAYER**

Gracious God, help us to rely on your strength when ours fails, and lean on your arms when ours grow weak. Amen.

Be merciful to me, LORD, for I am faint. O LORD, heal me, for my bones are in agony.

Psalm 6:2

## READ FOR REFLECTION

"You are old, father William," the
young man cried,
"And life must be hast'ning away;
You are cheerful and love to converse
upon death;
Now tell me the reason, I pray."

"I am cheerful, young man," father
William replied,
"Let the cause thy attention
engage;
In the days of my youth I
remember'd my God!
And He hath not forgotten my
age."

ROBERT SOUTHEY
(from "The Old Man's Comforts and How He Gained Them")

## MEDITATION

### *God Bless the Blue Thumb People*

We had gathered to listen to a representative of the Green Thumb organization. Founded after World War II, Green Thumb workers are past fifty-five years of age, and are recycled back into the world of work so that their talents and skills may still be used for the good of society.

After the presentation, John Steele, a retired Presbyterian minister, closed with prayer. Fervently he prayed that God would bless the Blue Thumb people. We all had a good laugh, but his slip of the tongue may have said more than he knew. The frailties of old age cause many blue thumb people. They are older people whose aging bodies have given way to the passing years, no longer able to function as in previous years. As older people live longer and receive medical care not available to previous generations, the number of blue thumb people will increase.

Garret Keizer tells about an elderly woman in his parish who got into a bathtub one day and couldn't get out. She pulled a towel from a rack, wrapped herself in it, and took a nap until some relatives found her, nearly dehydrated but calm. One of her great-granddaughters exclaimed, "Oh, Nana, it must have been so awful." Nana replied coolly from her bed, "You mean to tell me you spent four years away at college and never slept in a bathtub?"

 **PRAYER**

Lord, when our thumbs become blue,
Let us always turn to you. Amen.

# 23

"And there was a widow in that town who kept coming to him with the plea, 'Grant me justice against my adversary.' For some time he refused. But finally he said to himself, 'Even though I don't fear God or care about men, yet because this widow keeps bothering me, I will see that she gets justice.'"

Luke 18:3-5

## READ FOR REFLECTION

Widowhood is not an illness or disease, nor should it be regarded as a chronic condition or permanent status. It is a time of transition. . . . Regardless of one's age or any other circumstance, successful widowhood is coming away from bereavement not simply a full person, but one *fuller* than ever before.

ROBERT C. DI GIULIO

## *She Lives on a Street Full of Widows*

When I knocked at her door, I knew it would take her a few minutes to answer, for her steps were slow, and she managed only with a walker. We chatted for a while, and she let me know she lived on a street of widows. She told me that she can no longer go where she wants to go, that her life space has shrunk to just her modest house and sometimes a few rooms. She has learned to live alone, but her major fear is that the day will come when she has to leave her home. She let me know, "They will have to carry me kicking and screaming to a nursing home. I have learned to eke out whatever is left of life right here." I know that Annie is a feisty little lady and has clung to the last vestiges of her independence.

Annie reminded me of the widow in Jesus' parable, who begged the judge for justice against her adversary. Even though she had been rebuffed she persisted, and her continual pleading finally wore the judge down. Jesus used this parable to teach persistence in prayer.

In the days ahead there will be many more streets of widows. Any married woman faces weighted statistics that predict she will survive her mate. This is part of the mysterious chemistry of being a woman who carries longevity within herself. Annie reminds us that widows are our neighbors and our prized possessions, and their cries for justice need to be heard.

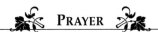 PRAYER

Loving God, thank you for widows who remind us that it takes persistence in our prayers to prevail. Amen.

# 24

So Rachel died and was buried on the way to Ephrath (that is, Bethlehem). Over her tomb Jacob set up a pillar, and to this day that pillar marks Rachel's tomb.

Genesis 35:19-20

## READ FOR REFLECTION

Marriage is the most intimate of life's many relationships. The bond between husband and wife can be deep, tender, and long-lasting. Thus the loss of our spouse can be one of life's most devastating emotional experiences. One half of us will have this experience, whether we wish it or not. It is the price of love.

R. SCOTT SULLENDER

## MEDITATION

### *The Widower's Plight*

The widower's plight? Yes, that's right. Now we can add that phrase to the widow's mite. It seems as if no one cares for or understands the special plight of the widower in our society. Some think that widowers are at a premium, sought after, deluged with invitations, and are not faced with the loneliness and isolation that widows experience. Nothing is further from the truth.

Jack is a widower, and for years has lived a lonely life at home. He sits in his favorite chair, listens to his police scanner, smokes incessantly, and stares at television. It seems that his life is measured by occasional trips to the post office and the drugstore. He says that all he wants is to end his days in his own home. In a room darkened by closed blinds he told me that life has never been the same since his wife died.

We are reminded of the patriarch Jacob who lost his wife Rachel. How he loved her! He had waited fourteen years before her father, Laban, would allow him to marry her. But it was worth it. The years seemed but a few days, the Bible says, because of the love he had for her.

The purest, sweetest thing in Jacob's life has been his love for this woman, and now the light of her face fades from his sight forever. Jacob remained a widower, no doubt living with his heartbreak until he died. Let us not forget the widower's plight.

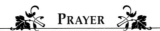 PRAYER

Friend of those who live alone, may they and we realize that being alone and in grief does not depend on gender. Amen.

# 25

Even to your old age I am he, even when you turn gray
I will carry you.                    Isaiah 46:4 (NRSV)

Surely he has borne our infirmities and carried our
diseases.                          Isaiah 53:4 (NRSV)

## READ FOR REFLECTION

Lord,
Your fingers never felt the trembling
    of old age,
whose skills diminish day by solemn day
    until
the deftness once defining who we are
    before the world
is lost.

You have not felt the weakness closing in
    upon your frame,
when stairs become too steep,
    words too softly spoken,
light too dim,
    or the familiar road
stretched long.

. . . . . . . . . . . . . . . . . . . . . . . . . . . . . . . . .

Yet you
speak to and for us in this shadowed vale, uttering
    "My God, why hast thou forsaken me?"
on our behalf, and pray
    "Forgive them; for they know not
what they do." And you
    commit our death-bound spirits, Lord, into
God's hands.

PEGGY L. SHRIVER
("An Aged Easter")

## *Did Jesus Ever Get Old?*

I was reading a Bible story to my six-year-old grandson, Christopher, when suddenly he looked at me and asked, "Grandpa, did Jesus ever get old?" I told him that Jesus only lived to be thirty-three, but that was old in those days. But his question made me wonder. Did Jesus know the frailties and illnesses of old age?

In his little book, *Stations of the Cross for Older Adults*, John van Bemmel raises the same concern: "God, your son never grew old. He can't teach us about getting old . . . about loneliness, about arthritis and failing eyesight."

I believe that on the cross Jesus experienced the diseases and infirmities of old age. On the way to the cross Jesus collapsed under the heavy wood, and although it was painful he got up and staggered to Calvary. He knew what it was like to be old and to fall down. He experienced loneliness, abandonment, and rejection at Calvary, common experiences for older people. He knew the painful feeling of remorse, over "what might have been," as do some older people who look back over their lives with regrets too deep for words.

Jesus could relate to the poor elderly, as he died with no possessions except the robe over which the soldiers gambled. Jesus may not have reached a chronological old age, but he experienced old age in his body on the cross.

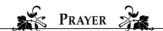 PRAYER

Ageless Christ, thank you for knowing what it feels like to be old. Amen.

# 26

The span of our life is seventy years—eighty for those who are strong—but their whole extent is anxiety and trouble, they are over in a moment and we are gone.

Psalm 90:10 (NJB)

## READ FOR REFLECTION

Abide with me; fast falls the eventide;
the darkness deepens; Lord, with me abide.
When other helpers fail and comforts flee,
Help of the helpless, O abide with me.

HENRY FRANCIS LYTE
("Abide With Me")

## *Preparing for Helplessness*

In "Preparing for Helplessness" William D. Auld writes that no one ever expects to be helpless, but some older persons face this. Therefore, while we still have some control over what happens to us, it is wise to plan ahead.

Auld raises four significant issues for which we need to prepare: (1) If I become helpless, where do I want to be living? (2) If I become helpless, who will care for me? (3) If I become helpless, who will handle my financial affairs? (4) If I become helpless, how will others know my wishes for medical care? Four excellent questions.

I asked a friend of mine, a widower, Auld's questions. At first he avoided them with nervous laughter and disclaimers that he was "not old enough" to be concerned about such matters. Later he called and told me that his financial affairs were in good shape, and he had already given copies of his "living will" to a durable power of attorney for health care. But the sensitive area was, "If I become helpless, where would I go, and who would take care of me?"

Since that initial conversation, we have had many talks about his future and what would happen if he did become helpless. It gave me the opportunity to suggest many alternatives should such a time come. Since many older persons will live thirty or more years past retirement, planning for the future is a wise move!

 **PRAYER**

Help of the helpless, strengthen, watch over, and help us as we plan our future. Amen.

So we do not lose heart. Even though our outer nature is wasting away, our inner nature is being renewed day by day.

2 Corinthians 4:16 (NRSV)

## READ FOR REFLECTION

There was once a young woman who visited the studio of the great artist Michelangelo. She was grieved to see him hacking away at the beautiful marble and argued with the illustrious sculptor and painter about what he was wasting. She pointed to the pile of chips that littered the floor. But Michelangelo said, "The more the marble wastes, the more the statue grows."

The years hack away the beauty of our bodies, but each part that time takes away unveils an inner being who is becoming more like Christ—the source and essence of all Christian life. Each stage in our lives is the beginning of a new aspect of Christian life. Our older age can be the beginning of our closest encounter with God.

LEO E. MISSINNE

## *The Spirit Grows As the Body Crumbles*

A small town drugstore was closing its doors after years of being the meeting place for many older persons. It had been a landmark of the town for years, and its closing brought a feeling of loss and sadness.

Its round tables and curlicue chairs provided hospitality for many older persons through the years. But today there was one special woman who caught my attention. She was bent over a table near the door, her back so badly twisted by arthritis that her face nearly touched the tabletop. Another aged lady came to say her good-byes to the old store, and soon the two began chatting about the old days at Dayvault's Drug Store.

They talked about the "good old days" when coffee wasn't colored water, and five-cent cones could be purchased in this very store, and when they had come here for after-school dates. Soon their conversation became a catalyst for others to reminisce, and her youthful spirit brought joy to everyone that day. Her body was crumbling away, but her spirit grew every day. She was bent over in her spine, but life had not bent her spirit.

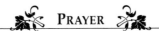 PRAYER

Gather my broken fragments to a whole
As these four quarters make a shining day.
Into thy basket, for my golden bowl,
Take up the things that I have cast away
In voice or indolence or unwise play.
Let mine be a merry, all-receiving heart,
But make it a whole, with light in every part. Amen.

George Macdonald

# 28

Do not cast me off in the time of old age;
Do not forsake me when my strength fails.

Psalm 71:9 (NKJV)

## READ FOR REFLECTION

The day becomes more solemn and serene
    When noon is past: there is a harmony
    In autumn, and a lustre in its sky,
Which through the summer is not heard or seen,
As if could not be, as if it had not been!

PERCY SHELLEY
("Hymn to Intellectual Beauty")

## *That Gets My Goat!*

We have often heard the old expression, "That gets my goat," but rarely understand the origin of this expression. It came from the stables of a race track. Wise trainers knew that they had to find a way to calm down the nervous horses before a race. So they put an old, plodding goat in the paddock with the horses. Somehow the placid, easy-going old goat would create a calming influence and quiet the horse. Competitors would try to win the race by stealing the goat. So the charge was made, "We lost the race because they got my goat!"

It is significant that we need the wisdom and calming influence of older persons in the fever of life. There is a certain peaceful maturity that older people can give. But, what gets my goat is the way some people still use ageist terms for older people, and continue to view us from the standpoint of physical decline.

One of the saddest aspects of old age is that many people are not aware of their soul's power over the aging body, and thus never develop their inner lives. The great German writer Goethe expressed the deep insight that in his younger years man lived through his body, whereas in old age he is forced to live against his body. The psalmist knew the source of his strength in old age. He cries to God, "Do not forsake me when my strength fails." God's presence can be like that old goat, bringing calm and confidence in the midst of our tensions.

 **PRAYER**

Friend of the aged, stay with us as we finish the race of life, and let nothing rob us of your presence. Amen.

# 29

The lookout reported, "He has reached them, but he isn't coming back either. The driving is like that of Jehu son of Nimshi—he drives like a madman."

2 Kings 9:20

## READ FOR REFLECTION

When young people are asked what they fear about getting old, they are likely to answer—loneliness, loss of physical health, loss of mental ability, fear of ending their days in a nursing home, etc. These fears are certainly experienced by older people, though perhaps not to the extent that young people imagine. But one older person's fear seldom considered by the young is the fear that seniors have of losing their driver's license.

I suspect this fear is more common among American seniors than older people in other countries. Nowhere else in the world are people as dependent upon their personal cars as in the United States. Nowhere else, in the developed nations at least, is the public transportation system so poor.

Even in this country, the urban elderly can survive nicely without a car. . . . But the picture is not nearly as bright for seniors living in rural areas, in suburbs, or in small cities and towns.

In these areas, having your own car is your ticket to independent living. Not having a car or a license to drive is to become dependent on other people. "It is," in one old man's poignant words, "the beginning of the end."

HANK MATTIMORE

## MEDITATION

### *When Your Driving Days Are Over*

Anyone who has seen the movie *Driving Miss Daisy* is aware that one of the sharpest blows to an older person's sense of dignity is the loss of a driver's license.

Fred, who loved to drive, experienced such loss. In his younger days some of his cronies called him, "Jehu," modeled after the biblical king who "drives like a madman." Everyone cringed at the thought of meeting old Fred on the highway, but no one could help but admire his indomitable spirit.

Eventually cancer and other illnesses took their toll, and he suffered intense pain. Despite his crippled condition, he still managed to take his old car out on the road, and enjoyed every trip. Despite the many crippling effects of painful arthritic knees, he amazed everyone by passing the driving road test in his eighty-first year. But the day finally came when he could no longer drive, and I saw the sadness in his eyes. He said, "I guess my driving days are over."

It wasn't long thereafter that cancer finally ended Fred's life. At his memorial service, I recalled his love of driving and pictured Fred driving a golden chariot down heaven's golden streets. Somehow this made his loss less painful.

 PRAYER

God who leads us, we pause to give thanks for your mercy and kindness to us on the roads of life. We know you never will forsake us or leave us . . . now or in the life to come. Amen.

# 30

We who are strong ought to bear with the failings of the weak and not to please ourselves. Each of us should please his neighbor for his good, to build him up.

Romans 15:1-2

## READ FOR REFLECTION

The only hope is in the simple fact that someone who dares to listen and to face the failing of life in its naked reality, will not run away but say with a word, a touch, a smile or friendly silence: "I know—you had only one life to live and it cannot be lived again, but I am here with you and I care."

HENRI J. M. NOUWEN

## MEDITATION

### *Annie's Little Red Wagon*

Annie told people she was in her early eighties, but no one really knew how old she was. She lived by herself, and whenever anyone from the church visited her, it seemed hours before she could stumble on her walker to unlock the door. She had had a hard life, overcoming alcoholism and a difficult marriage. She did not have many joyous memories or happy events to recall.

A few days before Christmas, half jokingly Annie told her minister, "All I want for Christmas is a little red wagon." When asked why, she replied, "Simple. So I can pull my groceries from the front door to the kitchen."

The next Sunday the minister preached about freeing the child in all of us at Christmas. He told the congregation about Annie and her wish for a little red wagon. He said her request exemplified the childlike heart . . . open innocence, creative excitement, and spontaneous wishes.

The following Sunday, Christmas Day, someone handed the minister a thank-you note to be read. The scraggly handwriting said: Thank all of you for the wagon and all your kindness. Love, Annie.

Annie's little red wagon filled her with joy. Once again wise people had brought gifts to a child.

 PRAYER

Loving Father, we praise you for thoughtful caregivers, who see the child in us. Amen.

# 31

Now we know that if the earthly tent we live in is destroyed, we have a building from God, an eternal house in heaven, not built by human hands.

2 Corinthians 5:1

## READ FOR REFLECTION

In his extreme old age, John Quincy Adams was slowly and feebly walking down a street in Boston. An old friend accosted him and, shaking his trembling hand, asked, "And how is John Quincy Adams today?"

"Thank you," said the ex-president. "John Quincy Adams is well, quite well, I thank you. But the house in which he lives is becoming quite dilapidated. It is tottering upon its foundations. Time and the season have nearly destroyed it. Its roof is pretty well worn out. Its walls are much shattered, and it trembles with every wind. The old tenement is becoming almost uninhabitable, and I think John Quincy Adams will have to move out of it soon. But he himself is quite well, quite well."

JOHN QUINCY ADAMS

## *He Himself Is Quite Well*

We had not seen Cecil for some time. It was somewhat of a shock to see his bent-over form and shuffling walk. My friend said, "He really has been broken by age, hasn't he?" Yet no one had such a contagious spirit as this man.

Paul likens the physical body to "an earthly tent," which will be destroyed. But he also is waiting for the moment when God will give him a new body, a spiritual body. Therefore, despite the flimsy tent in which he lives, he does not despair. William Barclay, in his commentary on Corinthians, states it well: "For, while we are in this tent of the body we groan, for life weighs us down, for it is not so much that we desire to be stripped of this house, but rather that we desire to put our heavenly body over it . . . So then we are always in good heart . . ." (2 Cor. 5:4, 6).

So, we need to resist the temptation to dwell on our physical decline. People grow old and weak in other cultures, some of which do not structure their understanding of aging in terms of physical decline. I like the positive spirit of former president John Quincy Adams, who even when he admitted his physical decline, could nevertheless affirm, "But he himself is quite well, quite well."

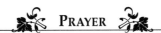 **PRAYER**

*Pray this ancient prayer of Saint Ignatius Loyola.*

Lord, teach me to serve thee as thou deservest . . .
> To give, and not to count the cost
> To fight, and not to heed the wounds
> To labor, and not to ask for rest save knowing that
I do thy will. Amen.

# IV

# When Your Best Is Good Enough

*What does it mean to show respect for or to be a credit to our elderly parents in today's complex, frenetic world? Does it mean that in the process of honoring them, we cease to honor ourselves? ... To honor thy father and mother ultimately means that we give up impossible, self-destructive expectations. Until we learn to honor ourselves, we cannot truly honor our elderly parents.*

*Vivian E. Greenberg*

But you say, "Whoever says to his father or mother, 'Whatever profit you might have received from me has been dedicated to the temple'—is released from honoring his father or mother." Thus you have made the commandment of God of no effect by your tradition.

Matthew 15:5-6 (NKJV)

## READ FOR REFLECTION

> I believe it was Erma Bombeck
> Who, remembering childhood,
> Told how her mother's extended arm
> Braced her in the automobile
> At sudden stops.
> Then one day Erma, the driver,
> Discovered herself supporting mother
> The same way.
> Foot touches brake,
> Strong arm touches weak arm,
> Love communicates its power,
> And insight is born.
> These are the role reversals
> That perpetuate the best
> In the human race.
>
> RONALD VAUGHAN
> ("Driving with Mother")

## *An Irredeemable Obligation*

Unlike some adult children in Jesus' day who tried to substitute religious duties for caring for aged parents, Margaret was a model of devotion for an aged parent. She denied her own needs to make sure her ninety-year-old mother had every comfort.

Margaret's husband watched in silence. Her children internalized their anger, or acted it out in school. Her own needs were never met. She felt she had an irredeemable obligation to her mother and arranged for her mother's every comfort. Church members praised her selfless love, and yet never offered any help. . . .

After her mother died, Margaret became a victim of Parkinson's disease. Her physician attributed her illness to stress and had no magic bullets to halt the disease. She suffered terribly, her face a blank mask of her former self, and she finally died in a nursing home at the age of sixty-seven.

There is little doubt that caring for aging parents will become more and more needed as people live into their eighties and nineties and beyond. May God provide the grace and strength to caregivers—who are often burdened to the point of exhaustion—and help them find a way to balance both the needs of their parents and their own.

 PRAYER

Understanding Lord, in our concern for our aging parents, may we not deny our own needs and right to happiness. Amen.

Moses' father-in-law replied, "What you are doing is not good. . . . The work is too heavy for you; you cannot handle it alone. . . . select capable men from all the people . . . and appoint them. . . . That will make your load lighter, because they will share it with you. . . . you will be able to stand the strain."

Exodus 18:17-18, 21-23

## READ FOR REFLECTION

We are given no training in being caregivers. People over the age of forty or fifty (the children of today's aged population) had no real examples to watch as they matured; no role models who would prepare them for the eventual job of being responsible for their own parents. . . .

HELEN HAYES

# MEDITATION

## *Many Demands/Much Stress*

An only son drives hundreds of miles every week to visit his aging mother, who lives alone and refuses to move in with either of her children. A business woman, with several teenagers at home, spends hours every week caring for her father in a nursing home. Yet he complains that his family has deserted him. After the death of their father, children quarrel over where mother will live, while she rigidly insists on staying where she is. These scenarios could be multiplied.

Moses found the burden of caring for the Israelites more than he could bear. As Jethro observed, he was not only wearing himself out, but the people's patience was wearing thin as well. His own well-being, as well as the good order of the community, was threatened. So Jethro advised Moses to delegate some of his responsibility to others, who would not only serve Moses well, but would bring peace to the people. Moses did not hesitate, and put the plan into effect. There is no doubt that sharing this burden with others prolonged Moses' leadership role in the community.

As friends and relatives of caregivers, may we provide the loving support and respite that these caretakers so desperately need. And as caregivers, may we adhere to Jethro's wisdom and realize that the work is too heavy for us to bear alone.

 PRAYER

Wonderful Counselor, grant us wisdom for facing this increasing issue of caring for our older parents. Amen.

But Ruth said, "Do not press me to leave you or to turn back from following you! Where you go, I will go; Where you lodge, I will lodge; your people shall be my people, and your God my God."

Ruth 1:16 (NRSV)

## READ FOR REFLECTION

*(A Letter to Caregivers)*

Dear Friends:

For the past seven years I have been in charge of the full care of my husband, John, who is now eighty-one years old. Every day *is* a labor of love. At first I felt much resentment that John was no longer himself, and hated the way in which he was slipping more and more away from me. . . .

Let me say to you that it is okay to feel angry when your patience wears out, or when some days are so hard you feel like you will explode. Don't feel guilty about having a "time out," or a time away from the stress. . . .

Learn to laugh at life. We have been married for fifty-seven years and are very close, yet the other day John said, "Why don't we get along?" Learn to see the person you care for as a person, not just a family member. More and more I am convinced of the truth of those words in scripture, "Nothing can separate us from the love of God."

Sincerely,
Isabelle Steele

## MEDITATION

### *She Cared for Katherine*

Anne's mother, Katherine, had been a chronic invalid for years. When she could no longer stay in her own apartment, there was no other alternative. By a mutual decision, Katherine moved to a rest home near Anne. It wasn't easy. Katherine's first words when she saw her room were, "Good Lord, has my life come to this?" Later some of her own furniture and pictures from the past made the room more livable.

Every day Anne, a teacher, would visit her mother after school. She knew the daily visits meant better care by the rest home. At first her mother complained constantly, and played the game of "divide and conquer" with threats of calling her son to take her to another place. Anne and her husband had to take vacations secretly, for if Katherine knew she would develop some sudden sickness.

A broken hip, mental confusion, and other issues added to Anne's burden. But the hardest thing to bear was the insensitivity of her brothers. Not only did they dump full responsibility on her, but they never expressed appreciation for her tireless care. Despite the stress, one redeeming feature was the closer relationship that did develop between Anne and her mother.

This story of caregiving is reminiscent of Ruth's care for her aged mother-in-law, Naomi. Rather than stay in Moab and expand her own options for the future, Ruth chose to stay with Naomi and care for her. Caregiving cannot be easily explained. It is an altruistic choice, an act of love which no rationale can explain.

 PRAYER

God who waits, when we choose to be caregivers for others, remind us how your care never ends. Amen.

# 35

Then God said, "Take your son, your only son Isaac, whom you love, and go to the region of Moriah. Sacrifice him there as a burnt offering on one of the mountains . . ."

Genesis 22:2

## READ FOR REFLECTION

For caregivers, finding inner strength is a matter of daily necessity. Their ability to endure often depends on having a solid awareness about why they are doing what they do. . . . Reaching for a spiritual view enlarges the day-to-day struggles of caregiving, placing them in a context in which it is possible to find meaning.

WENDY LUSTBADER AND NANCY R. HOOYMAN

## MEDITATION

### *When Caregiving Becomes a Burden*

The story of Abraham's intended sacrifice of Isaac has always intrigued me. Sacrificing Isaac would mean more than the death of a son he loved; it would mean to kill the promise, to sacrifice what alone seemed to make God's promise possible. Despite its difficulties, the story shows the obedience of a man prepared to live to the limit of the vision he possessed. In the end, God does not allow the sacrifice to happen, but provides a lamb for the sacrifice.

God does not intend for us to be sacrificed, like Isaac, on the altar of parents' needs.

What God does intend is for families to develop relationships of mutual giving and receiving across generations, to admit that all family members are weak and strong in different ways, and to allow members to ask for what each one needs and to give freedom to the other as they attempt to give.

We marvel at the faith of Abraham, but let us not forget the submission of Isaac who could have over-powered his older father. We marvel even more that God has provided the final sacrifice, Jesus Christ, and no one need ever give up his or her life for others.

 **PRAYER**

Caring God, you care for us in those long hours when we wear ourselves out caring for others. Help us to lean heavily on your everlasting arms. Amen.

# 36

When Jesus saw his mother there, and the disciple whom he loved standing nearby, he said to his mother, "Dear woman, here is your son," and to the disciple, "Here is your mother." From that time on, this disciple took her into his home.

John 19:26, 27

## READ FOR REFLECTION

Dear Heavenly Father,

You know the heavy responsibilities that daily weigh upon caregivers. We have valleys of self-doubt, depression, and chronic fatigue. There are sleepless nights and long days and a feeling of "no light at the end of the tunnel." We often ask ourselves how we can go on under such stress with no time for ourselves. Sometimes it is even difficult to leave our duties long enough to bathe or to sit down to rest for a brief time.

We know that Jesus had great compassion for the sick and suffering. May we follow His example and use our abilities and energy to continue our caregiving, confident that He is with us and will give us strength for the task if we put our hand in His. . . .

Dear Lord, when our period of caregiving is completed, may we remember others who are still struggling with this job and find ways to ease their burden. Amen.

(*Prayers for Caregivers*, Ginter Park Presbyterian Church)

## MEDITATION

### *Christ the Caregiver*

One of the most poignant moments in Jesus' life as a compassionate caregiver was his remembering his mother, Mary, from the cross. Despite his own agony and pain, he looked down and saw Mary, and had compassion on her. To the only disciple there, as is often the case, Jesus entrusted her care. "Dear woman, here is your son." John would care for his mother from that moment on.

In his dying hour, we see the heart and soul of his whole life. "The Son of Man did not come to be served, but to serve, and to give his life as a ransom for many" (Mark 10:45). He was the constant suffering servant who "took up our infirmities and carried our sorrows." Even in his extreme hour of pain and death, his thoughts went out to others.

Caregiving is no easy task. It means sacrificing one's own pastimes and plans for the good of someone else. Yet, the example of Jesus' care for his mother is our model and inspiration. During those long hours of caring, we need to realize that this job of caregiver is our service for God. The last stanza of "There Is a Green Hill Far Away" sums it well:

> O dearly, dearly has He loved,
> And we must love Him too,
> And trust in His redeeming blood,
> And try His works to do.

 PRAYER

Loving Lord, hold before us the constant example of your ceaseless love, your undying care for others. Amen.

Bear one another's burdens, and in this way you will fulfill the law of Christ. For all must carry their own loads.

Galatians 6:2, 5 (NRSV)

## READ FOR REFLECTION

The "bearing of burdens" is not something done simply "for" others; rather it is a corporate venture done "with" others since "each man will have to bear his own load" (Gal. 6:5). . . . It is a process whereby we listen with gentleness and patience, speak with truth and love, hold out a hand in times of loneliness and fear, sit in silence through the long night watches, and rejoice when the shadow of distress is dissolved in the warm sun of deliverance. . . .

There is throughout the basic intention of reestablishing broken relationships, of healing the wounds of loneliness and grief, of loving and forgiving in the context of truth and grace. There will always, of course, be things for the person to understand just as there will always be things to be done. But these are seen as derivative in the primary focus on encounter, on relationships, on reconciliation. The person is always more important than the problem, and the relationship is more important than the solution.

WILLIAM B. OGLESBY

## Bearing Burdens with Our Parents, Not for Them!

Paul asks us to bear burdens *with* others, not *for* them, and this is never more important than in our relationship to aging parents. How many times have you heard an older person say, "I just don't want to be a burden to my children." Despite some clever "guilt trips" that parents place on children, very few want to move in with their children or become a millstone around their children's necks.

It is difficult to really bear burdens *with* other people. Something in us makes us shy away from those who are suffering deeply, keeps us from those who need us most. We would rather say, "Amen," to Paul's further word that "all must carry their own load," for we feel ashamed, if not overwhelmed, by all the demands on us. How can we be expected to bear burdens with others if we cannot handle our own?

How do we resolve the paradox? We do need to share burdens *with* our parents, but, within limits, always giving them the freedom to make their own decisions and stay in control of their lives. And, even though sharing our burdens with others is helpful, we have to learn to bravely bear our own.

It is possible to deal with the demands on you and to share burdens *with* your older parents or relatives. But it is not easy and demands finding strength from a power greater than yourself. . . . The psalmist put it all in perspective, "Cast your burden on the LORD, and he will sustain you" (Psalm 55:22, NRSV).

 **PRAYER**

Gracious God, what would we do without the strength you give us to handle our own load and to bear burdens with others. Amen.

# 38

Greet Priscilla and Aquila, my fellow workers in Christ
Jesus. They risked their lives for me. Not only I but all
the churches of the Gentiles are grateful to them.

Romans 16:3-4

## READ FOR REFLECTION

On their golden wedding anniversary, a couple were
kept busy all day with the celebrations and the crowds
of friends and relatives who dropped in to congratulate
them. So they were grateful when, toward evening, they
were able to be alone on the porch, watching the sunset
and relaxing after the tiring day.

The old man gazed fondly at his wife and said, "Agatha,
I'm proud of you!"

"What was that you said?" asked the old lady. "You
know I'm hard of hearing. Say it louder."

"I said I'm proud of you."

"That's all right," she replied with a dismissive gesture.
"I'm tired of you, too."

ANTHONY DE MELLO

## MEDITATION

### *They Lived for Each Other*

Bill and Sybil grew older together. Their only son was killed in a tragic automobile accident twenty-five years ago. "We counted on him to take care of us in our old age," Sybil said. "But now all we have is each other." She added, "Wouldn't it be wonderful if the good Lord would just let us live and not age, and then take us home?"

They became caregivers to each other, each suffering some of the devastating illnesses of older age. The ravages of time had taken their toll. Their steps were slower, their memories dimmer, and their eyesight failing.

I confess I left their home with some feelings of sadness. Although my wife and I hope to remain independent as long as possible, we know we have children who will care for us if that time comes. But Bill and Sybil had no one . . . except each other. Yet I celebrated their closeness in their later years. They are models of a couple who have weathered the storm of the years and have found intimacy in the autumn of life.

They really did live for each other.

 PRAYER

God, who has placed the solitary in families, we pause now to say thanks for loved ones upon whom we can depend, but also pray for those who live alone as life winds down. Amen.

# 39

Then Eli realized that the LORD was calling the boy. So Eli told Samuel, "Go and lie down, and if he calls you, say, 'Speak, LORD, for your servant is listening.'"

1 Samuel 3:8-9

## READ FOR REFLECTION

In a way, not to be heard is not to exist. This can be the plight of the very young and the very old, the very sick, the "confused," and all too frequently the dying— literally no one in their lives has time or patience to listen. Or perhaps we lack courage to hear them.

MARGARET GUENTHER

## MEDITATION

### *Listening to One Another*

The story of the child, Samuel, and the aged priest, Eli, is a model of holy listening. Even the wise, experienced, and attentive Eli misses the point twice, but the Lord keeps on calling. Finally, Samuel learns to listen to his truest self, to the other, and ultimately to God.

How many times do we hear aging parents say, "Sit and talk with me. No one really listens to me anymore." Their security is bound up with the knowledge that their children will be there for them emotionally. What does that mean? It means that you will be there to listen to that person when she feels like talking.

Many older persons have suffered the loss of friends and miss that closeness. Others are often isolated from their church. So it does seem that adult children, with whom they have shared so many years of common experiences, can be their listeners. However, it is all too easy to tune out our parents because we are so close to them. At times we cannot "hear" what they are saying because of our own needs.

Holy listening to one another brings God's presence in new and strange ways. Because the young Samuel listened to the old Eli, he finally heard God's voice to him in the darkness. In that sense, holy listening is a living out of intercessory prayer.

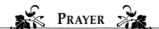 PRAYER

Our Father, who listens to us and our broken prayers, help us to really listen to others. Amen.

# 40

When King David was old and well advanced in years, he could not keep warm. . . . Then they . . . found Abishag, a Shunammite, and brought her to the king. . . . she took care of the king and waited on him . . .

1 Kings 1:1, 3-4

## READ FOR REFLECTION

Their concern was more than a personal one for King David, although they surely cared a great deal about him. But their larger concern was for their nation because a weak and failing king, it was believed, transferred his weakness to his subjects. The vitality and welfare of the kingdom were inseparable from the vigor of the monarch. Besides all that, they had their own jobs at stake. As David went, so they went. We can hardly blame them for taking every possible measure to keep David around for as long as they could.

KENNETH L. GIBBLE

## *Abishag: Unlikely Caregiver*

Abishag. What a strange story! We wonder why the writers of scripture included it. David's counselors were looking for a young woman to be his caregiver in his old age. It wasn't that David didn't have access to women—he had nine wives and many girlfriends—but none were present to care for him in his old age.

Kenneth Gibble claims that these counselors were acting on the ancient belief—or superstition—that a maiden had magical healing powers to cure senility or the feebleness associated with old age. Some translators of the text say that Abishag became the king's nurse. While we cannot resolve all the complexities of this ancient story, it has modern meaning for caring for older parents.

There comes a time when family and close friends cannot be the caregiver. Although over eighty percent of today's fragile elderly are maintained at home through the assistance of a family member, other caregivers are needed. The crucial question for the future remains, Who will care for us? In the future, when the percentage of older people needing care will double, the percentage of younger people—caregivers of the future—will sharply decline. Perhaps one answer lies in training caregivers who will ease the burden and allow older persons to remain in their homes without draining the life blood of their children.

Abishag appears for one brief moment on the stage of biblical history. She is an unknown caregiver. May her descendants be blessed!

 PRAYER

Wise God, give us the sense to know when we need to find unlikely caregivers to help us in our time of need. Amen.

# 41

Now five of them were wise, and five were foolish. Those who were foolish took their lamps and took no oil with them, but the wise took oil in their vessels with their lamps.

Matthew 25:2-4 (NKJV)

## READ FOR MEDITATION

In middle and late middle age you are still healthy and your children are grown up. *Now* is the time to prepare yourself and your children for old age and death.

SIDNEY CALLAHAN

MEDITATION

## *A Gift for the Next Generation*

There is no better gift we can give to the next genera-tion than to plan wisely for our old age and death. This is why the parable of the wise and foolish virgins speaks so directly to older persons. Although the time for the coming of the bridegroom was unknown, those who were wise were ready and prepared, while the foolish ones found themselves embarrassed by the moment.

No one knows for sure when the debilities of old age and death will become our experience. But Jesus' parable teaches us that unless we prepare beforehand, we cannot be prepared at all. Some things simply are not possible to get ready at the last minute.

It is important to face these issues now, however painful that may be, before frailty and debilitating illnesses put the burden on our adult children who are often unsure about their parents' wishes. Two blessings follow. We are given the dignity of owning our decisions, and our children are relieved of that responsi-bility and can carry out their parents' wishes without fear or guilt.

The foolish ones could not borrow oil in the hour of need. When the hour of destiny arrived, they were too late, and the door was closed. Settling matters now about our old age and death is a gift we give the next generation. As we move on with dignity into our remaining days, may we seek God's wisdom before we hear that midnight cry.

 PRAYER

God of hope, help us to face our future and plan for it, always realizing that we are given your help and presence. Amen.

# 42

You are those who have stood by me in my trials.

Luke 22:28

## READ FOR REFLECTION

Becoming a successful caregiver means becoming a person who fully accepts the responsibility not just for her [or his] own life, but for someone else's life as well.

PATRICIA BROWN COUGHLAN

## *When Life Tumbles In*

Their lives changed after the fall. For him, it meant a never ending struggle against the effects of his illness. For her, it meant a long, twilight struggle to be his primary caregiver and yet maintain her stressful role as a church executive. She was in the unenviable position of being the person for her frail husband and yet bearing the burden of many others.

She spent all her energies and time with him in the hospital, while he battled back from near death. As someone said, "She would not let him die." On one occasion she told me that her constant presence with her husband was essential, for too many ignored the needs of an older man. She spoke with clarity about receiving care from others. She who had been a caregiver to so many, now found herself the recipient of care. I am sure she wished it were the other way, but she told me she rejoiced that there were those who can and did help bear their burdens.

She helped me realize the importance of continued care. "So many people came at first; it was overwhelming," she said. "But later on, when the crisis abated, the number got fewer and fewer." I thought of Jesus' words about his closest disciples. "These are they who have stood by me in my trials." Sometimes in our haste to condemn the disciples for their flight at the Crucifixion, we forget the constancy of their love for the Master those many years. True caring means continued support.

 PRAYER

Lord, we pray for constancy in our caring. Amen.

# V

# Where Time Stands Still

*I have been in enough nursing homes for enough years to become a part, a participant in a world of unexplained noises and strange sights, odd appearances and mysterious events, which at their heart are the most mundane of things. Nursing homes hold all the force and drama of life and death and the movements between, made manifest in earthly banality.*

Sallie Tisdale

# 43

The woman came and knelt before him. "Lord, help me!" she said. He replied, "It is not right to take the children's bread and toss it to their dogs." "Yes, Lord," she said, "but even the dogs eat the crumbs that fall from their masters' table."

Matthew 15:25-27

## READ FOR REFLECTION

Too many Christians (and their families) act as if the nursing home bears a sign on the door that reads, "Abandon hope, all ye who enter here." If you truly believe that God is everywhere, then He is surely as present in nursing homes as He is in your own home. God will not abandon your parent at the door of the nursing home; He's going right in there with her.

BARBARA DEANE

## *Just a Few Crumbs Please!*

As we shared favorite Bible stories from the life of Jesus, Gladys chimed in, "My favorite story is the one with the woman begging for crumbs from the table." When we appeared baffled, she went on. "You know . . . that woman whom Jesus seemed to rebuke, but she didn't quit. All she wanted was a few crumbs from the table."

Belah added, "She had more faith than the disciples who wouldn't admit God's love could be found in an outsider. I often feel like an outsider in this nursing home. Like that woman, I would settle for a few crumbs of kindness."

I pondered her words a long time. I saw that long line of wheelchairs in the hall with persons staring into an endless silence. I saw the sadness of people who wait for visitors that never come. I saw those with faces that expressed "I'm waiting to die."

Residents of nursing homes want to be recognized and affirmed, not patronized or called by their first names without permission. Maggie sits by the nurses' station with her bags packed to go home. Oscar paces the hall, asking for something "to do." Pete takes out his railroad watch and endlessly checks the time. Martha sits with that glazed look, not knowing who or where she is.

Crumbs of kindness from our table, crumbs of compassion from our laden tables—that's all they ask. As Jesus gave in to the woman, so we, too, must reach out to these forgotten people.

 **PRAYER**

Loving God, a crumb from your table is better than a feast from others. Amen.

# 44

For my soul is full of trouble and my life draws near the grave. I am counted among those who go down to the pit; I am like a man without strength.

Psalm 88:3-4

## READ FOR REFLECTION

Many illnesses deprive a person only of the *present*. . . . Alzheimer's disease, however, robs the sufferer not only of the present and the future, but also of the past, as all memory of prior events, relationships, and persons slips away.

STEPHEN SAPP

## MEDITATION

### *When Alzheimer's Disease Strikes*

Martha is in the second phase of Alzheimer's disease. After going through a "forgetful" stage, she is now so confused that she cannot even remember her grand-children's names or her own address. Although robust in body, her mental state is becoming more disoriented, and soon will reach the third stage of "dementia" when she can no longer be left alone, and may be sent to live in the strange, frightening environment of the nursing home.

Her sense of the past has been blurred, and Martha finds it difficult to pray. Her experience mirrors that of the psalmist who went through an extended period of serious illness during which he was forced by the slow ebb of his physical powers to realize the loss of his relationship with God. For the psalmist "darkness had become his closest friend."

Alzheimer's disease, with its physical deterioration and loosened social relationships can separate a person from God. As Glenn Weaver says, "[it] produces chaos in the part of the body that is most central to our imaging of God in this life."

Yet, our Christian faith reminds us that even when our experience makes us feel very distant from God, the work of the Spirit in believers keeps us in the life of Christ, so that ". . . nor any other created thing shall be able to separate us from the love of God which is in Christ Jesus our Lord."

 **PRAYER**

Help us to realize that even when you seem so distant and removed from us, Lord, we are never outside your love and care. Amen.

It is for us who are strong to bear with the susceptibilities of the weaker ones, and not please ourselves. Each of us must consider his [or her] neighbour's good, so that we support one another.

Romans 15: 1-2 (NJB)

## READ FOR REFLECTION

> Live thy Life,
>     Young and old,
> Like yon oak,
> Bright in spring,
>     Living gold;
>
> Summer-rich
>     Then; and then
> Autumn-changed,
> Soberer-hued
>     Gold again.
>
> All his leaves
>     Fallen at length,
> Look, he stands,
> Trunk and bough,
>     Naked strength.

ALFRED, LORD TENNYSON
("The Oak")

## MEDITATION

### *At the Edge of the Cliff*

One of my former students, Kevin Burns, tells this story of working as an assistant at a nursing home. Every day he would help Cliff to get from his bed to a wheelchair, so he could go and visit his wife, Zora. Every day Cliff's spirit took on new life as he went to his wife's room. Her condition was worse than his, as her shriveled body was unable to move from her bed. But she could talk, and for a few shining moments they held their wrinkled hands, and shared their lifelong love.

When he wasn't with his wife, Cliff would sit alone at the end of the hall. Nursing assistants were too busy to talk with him. The only attention he got was when he couldn't control his bladder, and a nursing assistant had to change his pants. He complained that no one in that place cared for him, except his wife.

One morning Cliff refused to leave his bed. When asked if he wanted to see Zora, he screamed with undirected anger, "Zora's dead!" All attempts at cheering him up failed. The spirit of the old man with the crushed body was gone. . . . He had no will to live. His only words were, "You gotta gun so I can kill myself?"

Many persons in nursing homes share Cliff's sentiments. They are friendless, helpless, and hopeless. Paul exhorts the strong to help the weaker ones. . . .

What can you do today to "stop one heart from breaking?"

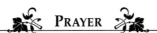 **PRAYER**

Friend of the friendless, let us remember in prayer those on the edge of the cliff, waiting for death to be their release. Amen.

# 46

But at once he spoke to them and said, "Courage! It's me! Don't be afraid." Then he got into the boat with them and the wind dropped.

Mark 6:50, 51 (NJB)

## READ FOR REFLECTION

We seemed dead
in our restraints;
now, we arise
from gerichairs
asking the time.
Tell the curious
at the door
a young physician,
late of Nazareth,
appeared to say:
"Unbind them!
Let them live!"

WESLEY F. STEVENS
("Miracle at Bethany Nursing Home")

## *We're All in the Same Boat Here*

Ruby was a newcomer to the group of nursing home residents. A few days ago, she had left her home, no longer able to live alone. She seemed forlorn and woebegone, and sat in stony silences as tears slithered down her aged cheeks.

Pauline read the story of Jesus coming to the disciples at three in the morning during a violent storm. They had struggled against adverse winds and felt overwhelmed and defeated. But Jesus got into their boat and calmed their fears.

Pauline turned to Ruby and said, "I know it's hard to leave your home and come here. But we're all in the same boat here. We'll help you through this, and never forget, Jesus gets into this boat with us." A glimmer of hope peeked through Ruby's gloom as she mustered a faint smile.

At the moment of facing displacement and dislocation, at the edge of panic and despair, God gets into the boat with us, and we find others there, too. Now, we can bear the unbearable and live.

 PRAYER

God who sits with us, we praise you for never leaving us to our fears, even when the storms come and our boat is so small. Amen.

# 47

Now write down for yourselves this song and teach it to the Israelites and have them sing it. . . . So Moses wrote down this song that day and taught it to the Israelites.

Deuteronomy 31:19, 22

## READ FOR REFLECTION

Music therapy captured the attention of members of the U. S. Senate and prompted a congressional hearing a few years ago. The witnesses were doctors, famous musicians, and a ninety-year-old resident of a nursing home who said, "Music is better than medicine."

HARRY F. ROSENTHAL

## *For Some, Music Is Better Than Medicine*

Randall had been coming to the worship services at the nursing home, but he sat in his wheelchair, stock-still and staring into space. On this occasion, as we sang the old song, "Jesus Loves Me! This I Know," we noticed his hands were moving ever so slightly, as if in time with the music. Suddenly *he* began to sing along . . . "Little ones to him belong; they are weak, but he is strong." The first time he had ever spoken in that place.

The scene is repeated differently thousands of times a day. Music is the universal language of the soul, and at times the only stimulus to which older people respond. There is something about the old hymns of the church that causes older persons—disabled by Parkinson's and Alzheimer's disease and strokes—to respond.

David used music therapy with King Saul. When he played on the lyre, it seemed to soothe Saul's depression. The song found in Deuteronomy 32 was to remind Israel of their faith in God. "He is the Rock, his works are perfect, and all his ways are just. A faithful God who does no wrong" (Deut. 32:4).

Music therapy not only soothes the depression of older people, but serves as a catalyst to remind us of God's faithfulness and love.

Let the sounds of music fill the corners of nursing homes.

 PRAYER

Thank you, God, that music restores the soul. Amen.

# 48

Then he took a cup, and after giving thanks he gave it to them, saying, "Drink from it, all of you; for this is my blood of the covenant, which is poured out for many for the forgiveness of sins."

Matthew 26:27-28 (NRSV)

## READ FOR REFLECTION

Sunday afternoon at a local nursing home—not our town's best. . . .

Suddenly, into the chapel, wandered an Alzheimer's patient. Before anyone could stop her, confused, she rushed to the holy table. With one sweep of her arm she knocked off the tray of Communion wine.

Disaster! A sickening noise as it hit the floor and the tiny glasses tumbled out, spilling into a great, crimson gush that kept spreading.

Afterwards, strangely, I felt almost glad this catastrophe had happened. Communion that afternoon seemed less perfunctory, more precious. Why?

Because the cross itself shocked bystanders something like that. Surely Calvary evoked similar gasps of disbelief and pain from those followers of Jesus who witnessed it. And from the Victim.

"My God, my God, why have you forsaken me?"—The dreadful lament brings us up short. We can only pause and let the horror sink in. Left to death! The nauseating, crimson gush widens, nearly drowns us.

DWYN MECKLIN MOUNGER

## MEDITATION

### *Spilt Wine/Sudden Blessing*

Strange things do happen at communion services in nursing homes. Gnarled hands unable to hold the communion bread. Nurses interrupting the service to give medicine. One obviously hungry resident who kept saying to the minister, "Give me some more of that bread." But none more significant than the day Dr. Mounger described when the Alzheimer's patient spilled the communion wine.

The spilt wine became a sudden blessing as it recalled the poured out life blood of Jesus. His cry of dereliction touches us as we face some of life's crises and agonies. When we feel abandoned and forsaken, we take comfort that Jesus experienced that too, and in such a way that no one else need ever know that final desolation.

Dr. Mounger concludes, "The Word of God that still rings out! The reassuring word that Christ gasped the very same wrenching sob. The Good Friday invitation to pause, to gaze at the spilled crimson that is our healing, our only hope, our glory."

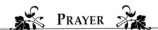 **PRAYER**

O sacred Head, now wounded, With grief and shame
  weighed down,
Now scornfully surrounded With thorns, thine only
  crown.
O sacred Head, what glory, What bliss till now was
  Thine!
Yet, though despised and gory, I joy to call Thee mine.
  Amen.

# 49

And so Jesus also suffered outside the city gate to make the people holy through his own blood. Let us, then, go to him outside the camp, bearing the disgrace he bore.

Hebrews 13:12-13

## READ FOR REFLECTION

Dare to believe you have a facility that is a place of life with energy to give. The awareness and cultivation of that spiritual energy doesn't just happen. It happens when those in charge of nursing homes become determined to stop the image of the home as a place to be pitied and avoided.

JAMES A. CAMPBELL

## *Going Outside the City Gate*

Whenever I want to rediscover the real meaning of Christian love, I visit someone in a nursing home. Here are real souls existing in a place most avoid; often subject to disgraces words cannot describe. Henri Nouwen refers to an old legend in the Talmud which tells about the coming of the Messiah. When Rabbi Yoshua ben Levi came upon the prophet Elijah he asked him, "When will the Messiah come?" Elijah replied that he is "sitting at the gates of the city . . . sitting among the poor covered with wounds."

So many wounded souls sit in darkness and the shadow of death in these never ending halls and rooms of nursing homes. Some sit in shock, still trying to recover from being placed there. Others deal with the loss of control, and the endless search for meaning in that place. Still others desperately crave a deeper spiritual life. As one resident said, "When you come to a place like this, your faith is your support. Only God sees you through here."

All need to be affirmed and valued. In my first days as a chaplain in a nursing home I often despaired of ever knowing one person from another. Old and frail, they lined the corridors, and like prisoners or refugees, they all looked alike. When I began to affirm them as persons, listen to their stories, be present in their lives, I knew the presence of One who "died outside the city wall." Here the Lord can still be found, offering His wounds to heal the wounds of others.

 PRAYER

Suffering God, help us to find your presence among the poor, covered with wounds. Amen.

# 50

Rejoicing in hope, patient in tribulation, continuing steadfastly in prayer.

Romans 12:12 (NKJV)

## READ FOR REFLECTION

Jesus' disciples were asking a very ordinary, straight-forward and legitimate question when they asked the teacher to teach them to pray. To the extent that new residents of nursing homes want pastoral care, that is the question that they are asking: Teach us to pray, to develop the inner side of our lives of devotion so that we can live through to assurance, to the re-creation of a meaningful life, and to a new relationship with God.

HENRY C. SIMMONS

## *Where Learning to Pray Again Is a Priority*

We listened as Cleta shared feelings about her life in the nursing home. "All my life I prayed in church and at home, but since coming here I have had to learn to pray all over again." She went on, "When I first came here I felt so worthless. I wanted to be doing something. I felt like an old, sagging sweater, all worn out and good for nothing, with no hope of getting better."

Life in a nursing home is reminiscent of the way the Hebrew exiles felt by the waters of Babylon. When their captors asked them to sing one of the songs of Zion, they replied, "How shall we sing the Lord's song in a strange land?" Praising God in Babylon was far different than hymns and prayers offered in Jerusalem.

Nursing home residents need to learn again how to pray in their own "strange land." They can discover that prayer is loving energy sent out into the world. Prayer is a way of being with others even when they feel captive to their confinement.

Cleta shared with the rest of the group that she now had more time for prayer and quiet waiting in the presence of the Lord. She concluded, "I guess that's one reason the good Lord has left me here so long. I need to spend more time with Him." She had a beauty of soul which touched us all.

 PRAYER

Help us, O God, to realize that we begin to pray when life closes in on us, and we face loneliness of soul. Amen.

# 51

A friend is a friend at all times, it is for adversity that a brother [or sister] is born.

Proverbs 17:17 (NJB)

## READ FOR REFLECTION

There is a phrase of Shakespeare's that, for me, perfectly describes friendship in Christ:

> Those friends thou hast, and their adoption tried,
> Grapple them to thy soul with hoops of steel.

Steel is apt for the enduring strength of such friendships. Hoops will do nicely to stand for roundness, the circle of perfection that draws us together in Christ.

EMILIE GRIFFIN

## *Old Friends*

Who of us will forget that memorable scene from the movie *Driving Miss Daisy* when Hoke, her chauffeur, tries to calm Miss Daisy when she is bewildered and confused. She pays him a high compliment when she says, "Hoke, you are my best friend."

Friends are particularly important as we grow older. We lose some of them by death or geographical distance. For those remaining, friendship becomes a sacrament with deep meaning.

I have often wondered if Simeon and Anna, the two older persons who experienced the Christ child, were old friends. No doubt their long hours of service in the temple led to spiritual friendship, and what greater bond than being present at the dedication of the Messiah.

Tracy Kidder's novel, *Old Friends*, tells of the friendship between Lou Freed and Joe Torchio, strangers thrust together as roommates in Linda Manor, a nursing home. The author says, "The central problem of life at Linda Manor is, after all, the universal problem of separateness: the original punishment, the ultimate vulnerability, the enemy of meaning."

Lou and Joe develop a friendship that transcends all the indignities and impersonal life of the nursing home. Their story reminds us that there is no greater gift someone can give a person in a nursing home than to be his or her friend.

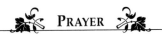 PRAYER

Thank you, Father, for sending people into our lives to be our friends. May we appreciate them and honor their memory when they leave us. Amen.

Continue to love each other like brothers, and remember always to welcome strangers, for by doing this, some people have entertained angels without knowing it.

Hebrews 13:1 (NJB)

## READ FOR REFLECTION

In the letter to the Hebrews we are not only encouraged to love one another, but admonished always to welcome strangers. It seems that some who have done this have entertained angels unaware. . . .

The appearance of an angel would [probably frighten] most of us out of our wits. We would [possibly be] more at ease with a stranger.

It may be that this is the reason that all of the angels I have ever known have first appeared to me as strangers. Only later, after getting to know them better, did I discover they possessed those attributes that qualified them as messengers from the Lord God. After they got through being strangers and started being angels, it was no time at all until they were recognized as the kind of friends you would never want to be without. There are a lot more angels, who, in the beginning, look like strangers than one might think. The next time you are in the presence of a stranger extend the warmest greeting you can muster. Who knows when an angel might be about?

MARTIN PIKE

## MEDITATION

### *An Angel Unaware*

The moment I walked into her room at the nursing home she welcomed me with a warm smile. In a creaky voice she told me she would be a hundred years old soon, but she said, "I can't remember if I was born in 1895 or 1896." Her ageless fingers pointed to an old desk, where a faded photo album told her story. "That's me," she said, "A long time ago when I was human."

She praised her sons who had cared for her, but with gentleness lamented the fact that so few church members visited her. Her sadness reminded me of that classic answer of the little girl who, when asked by her Sunday School teacher why the priest and Levite had bypassed the man on the road, replied, "Because they saw he had already been robbed!"

I departed with a prayer, and she said, "You are an angel." "No," I replied, "You are an angel. We met as strangers, but you have been a messenger from God."

As Americans grow grayer and grayer, there will be more and more like this gentle woman—older women living beyond ninety, often alone, forgotten, crying inside. Let us not forget that these strangers in nursing homes may be angels.

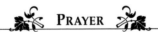 **PRAYER**

Host of the stranger, may we discover that strangers may become angels without our knowing it. Amen.

# 53

So then, putting away falsehood, let all of us speak the truth to our neighbors, for we are members of one another.

Ephesians 4:25 (NRSV)

## READ FOR REFLECTION

Get this scene straight in your mind: The Lord God of all creation comes to Abraham and says, in whatever way the Lord God speaks, "Abraham, you shall have a son!"

Now Abraham was not born yesterday. He had been around. But dutifully, he fell on his face. Even so he could not contain himself, and the Bible says, "he laughed." When he answered the Lord, he actually changed the subject!

And remember when Sarah heard the same prophecy, she laughed, too! . . .

Such were the honest responses of two aged disciples who had enough life experience to know when something was downright funny. They knew, as well, that what was being talked about here required a miracle . . .

So we see that in a very remarkable way, the redemption of the world actually begins with the laughter of old people!

RONALD VAUGHAN

## MEDITATION

### *That Refreshing Honesty*

Anyone who has worked in a nursing home, or visited people there, know this is the one place people are honest! Whether by age or medication, residents are freed from the need to weigh every word and the opinion of others, and they usually "tell it like it is!"

In one of my attempts to preach at a chapel service, I muttered a few finely polished phrases, and one lady, sitting near the front, shouted, "This is the nearest to nothing I ever heard in my life. I'm leaving!" Whereupon she wheeled out of the chapel, taking half the congregation with her.

On another occasion, the visiting minister had spoken too long, and when he finally finished he said, "It has been a pleasure being with you today, and I will return soon." One disgruntled man said, "I sure hope not."

Then there was the time when I led the group in singing the old hymns, and since the lights were so bright I turned them off. An irate woman loudly protested, "If you want me to sing, you'll have to turn those lights back on."

We laugh at these remarks, and yet wonder if there is not some real truth here. We still live in a plastic world where we wear masks to protect ourselves from others. Isn't it refreshing to know that honesty still can be found, even if in the blunt words of persons in a nursing home?

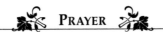 **PRAYER**

Lord of truth, help us to learn from those whom we often ignore or patronize, that we can be honest. Amen.

# VI

# *Harvested Wisdom*

*Now that the harvest is gathered and you stand in the autumn of your life, your oar is no longer a driving force carrying you over the oceans of your inner and outer worlds, but a spirit of discriminating wisdom, separating moment by moment the wheat of life from the chaff, so that you may know in both wheat and chaff their meaning and their value in the pattern of the universe.*

*Helen Luke*

# 54

And they spoke to him, saying, "If you will be a servant to these people today, and serve them, and answer them, and speak good words to them, then they will be your servants forever." But he rejected the counsel which the elders gave him, and consulted the young men . . .

1 Kings 12:7-8 (NKJV)

## READ FOR REFLECTION

The Orient reveres age. The Occident disparages it. In the East the assumption seems to be that one is born without knowledge or wisdom, both of which come by maturity and experience. One learns to live by living; and the longer one lives, the likelihood of his understanding and insight deepens. Wisdom is the garnered harvest of the years. . . .

Modern society has not learned the folly exemplified in Rehoboam, the son of King Solomon, who "rejected the advice which the elders had given him and spoke to the people as the young men had advised." The advice of the young turned out to be folly, and plunged his nation into a senseless civil war, whereas the counsel of the old was unquestionable wisdom. We need voices summoning us to respond to the counsel of the ancient biblical writer [of Leviticus 19:32] who proposed: "Rise in the presence of [the aged, show respect for the elderly] . . ." We need to be reminded of the psalmist's judgment that "the righteous . . . still bear fruit in old age."

DONALD G. MILLER

## *The Peril of Ignoring Wisdom*

The biblical story of King Rehoboam ignoring the counsel of his elders proves the valuable wisdom of elders. In deciding how to govern his new kingdom, Rehoboam turned to the elders who counseled compassion; they advised the king to be a servant to the people. Instead, he went with the advice of the young men who wanted a heavier yoke, a spiked lash, a policy of severity and servitude.

Rehoboam's rejection of elder wisdom plunged the nation into needless rebellion and civil war. He discounted the garnered wisdom of experience and made expediency his agenda. That unfortunate choice created division and final defeat.

As I move ever closer to my seventieth year, I admit to some queasy feelings that old age may finally have caught up with me. I don't want to go soulless into that dark night. I dread the thought that my final days on this earth will be diminished by nothingness, or dribbled away in nonsense. So the wisdom of those who have aged with grace, who possess remarkable vitality and ageless spirit, mean more and more to me.

It is not enough for society to make older persons comfortable or fulfill physical needs. We must honor their wisdom and call upon them as mentors in this generation. We wonder what might have happened if Rehoboam had not shunted his elders aside and had listened to their counsel!

 PRAYER

Mighty Fortress, help us to respect those who have fought enough battles to know what the warfare of life is all about. Amen.

# 55

> Length of days is not what makes age honourable, nor number of years the true measure of life; understanding, this is grey hairs, untarnished life, this is ripe old age.
>
> Wisdom of Solomon 4:8-9 (NJB)

## READ FOR REFLECTION

Old age is not all pain and limitations. It holds its own joys and satisfactions. The time has come when musing replaces activities—when the sleepless hours are filled with the harvest of a well-stored mind. Even though our means are scant, we know that our material needs will, somehow, be met.

POLLY FRANCIS

---

*Wisdom of Solomon is found in the Apocrypha in Protestant translations of the Bible.

## MEDITATION

### *Wanda's Wisdom*

At age 102, she was pushed in her wheelchair into a large assembly hall to share with us some of the garnered wisdom of her years. She called it, "Threads in the Fabric of Life."

"Joy must be distinguished from happiness," she said. "Happiness is fleeting, but joy is permanent. We find joy in every circumstance of life."

Her second thread was light. She said, "The light of faith must be nourished throughout life, the threads woven into life in such a way that none are broken by the hardships we undergo. We must always keep faith in the good and true."

Finally she spoke about love. With amazing preciseness she rattled off the different Greek words for love, and concluded, "the highest is *agape*, God's love bestowed on us. At age 102, looking back on my life, all that remains are those special moments when God's love shone into my life, and I knew I was loved." What wisdom from this centenarian!

 **PRAYER**

Loving God, may we find joy, light, and love in these older years. Amen.

# 56

Remember the days of old; consider the generations long past. Ask your father and he will tell you, your elders, and they will explain to you.

Deuteronomy 32:7

## READ FOR REFLECTION

Old age hath yet his honour and his toil;
Death closes all: but something ere the end,
Some work of noble note, may yet be done,
. . . . . . . . . . . . . . . . . . . . . . . . . . . . . . . . . . . .
Though much is taken, much abides; and though
We are not now that strength which in old days
Moved earth and heaven; that which we are, we are;
One equal temper of heroic hearts,
Made weak by time and fate, but strong in will
To strive, to seek, to find, and not to yield.

ALFRED, LORD TENNYSON
(from "Ulysses")

## *From Ageism to Sageism*

In other cultures and at earlier times in our own country, people looked forward to growing old. For them, old age was life's crowning stage and elders were considered blessed with unique wisdom and special powers. Both in New England and in the southern colonies, *eldershippe* was widely observed in the governance of church and state. People generally agreed that "gray heads" were wiser than "green ones," as Increase Mather put it.

In his farewell speech to the new generation of Israelites, Moses cautioned them to seek the counsel of the elders. Today, we are beginning to make a significant transition from ageism to sageism. Older people are beginning to be once again revered as elders, with wisdom garnered from experience.

Rabbi Zalman Schachter-Shalomi sees the last stages in the life cycle as a time for harvesting what has been learned and experienced. As he says, "When you are working on a computer, sometimes you type a whole page and then the power goes out. If you have not saved your work to a disk, it is all lost. A lifetime asks the same question, 'Are you saved?' You must write into the global awareness what it is you have accumulated in your lifetime and who you have become." To paraphrase some words of Moses, "I wish that all the LORD'S people were sages, and that the LORD would put His spirit upon them!" (Num. 11:29).

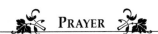 PRAYER

God of wisdom, help us to "save our past," by sharing our wisdom and mentoring the next generation. Amen.

Stand at the crossroads and look; ask for the ancient paths, ask where the good way is, and walk in it.

Jeremiah 6:16

## READ FOR REFLECTION

*(This is a fable.)*

The Children of Israel had been turned back from the Promised Land because they had not been faithful to the Spirit of God. Now, they were wandering, slowly, through the Wilderness, seeking out what sustenance they could.

This was a problem for the Children of Israel, for there were so many of them—more than 500,000 men plus women and children. . . .

Because of all the problems involved in feeding so vast a multitude, the leaders had to find some way of easing the load. So they decreed that everyone over sixty-five years of age must be left to die in the Wilderness, forgetting, of course, how soon they would reach that age. That immediately eliminated half the population, as people in those days often lived to be 120 or 130 years old. . . .

The remnant of the Children of Israel continued to wander in the Wilderness, but soon forgot why and where they were going. One day a child asked, "Where are we going?" No one could answer. . . .

The Children of Israel were never heard from again. They are called the Lost Tribes of Israel because they no longer had any older people to show them the way.

ROBERT GIEZENTANNER

## MEDITATION

### *Take Time to Listen to Wisdom*

Mae is a retired schoolteacher and supervisor of curriculum. For over forty years she taught and inspired people in the life of learning. Her husband, Howard, told me that she often had to walk three miles to her one-room schoolhouse where she taught six grades. He added, "There were times when I had to take her to school on horseback when the winter snows were too deep to manage."

Mae's hearing is gone, but her mind is alert and active. It may be a blessing that visitors have to curtail their speech because then they can listen to her wisdom. She is a deeply spiritual person and well versed in the Bible. Those who visit her never leave without a blessing.

Once we were discussing prayer in old age, and Mae remarked, "Prayer becomes harder, not easier in old age. Only if the seeds of a vital prayer life are sown early will it flower in old age." How true! What abundance of spiritual wisdom can be found in many older people if we just take the time to visit them and listen to them.

 PRAYER

Our constant Friend, we thank you for a lifetime of knowing your presence, which becomes even more real as life winds down to its end. Amen.

# 58

At Joppa there was a certain disciple named Tabitha, which is translated Dorcas. This woman was full of good works and charitable deeds which she did.

Acts 9:36 (NKJV)

## READ FOR REFLECTION

Each of us has a mission to accomplish in the name of Christ. We have no way of knowing when the important moment may arrive. Perhaps it will come in these twilight years. Responsible initiative allows us to weave the texture of our days.

MARY HESTER VALENTINE

## *The Unveiling of McGranny*

Wesley Stevens, Director of Holly Hall Retirement Community in Houston, Texas, relates the amazing story of Angie Runnels. Born the ninth of ten children, her father died when she was seven years of age. After marriage she bought a saddle horse and took over the job of driving away wild horses and cows from the open country where Angie settled. For years she served meals to oil field workers in her home, and later she ran a catering business.

At the age of eighty-four she moved into Holly Hall, and although legally blind, she used a special machine to read. But her love was still feeding people.

At the age of ninety-one her car broke down outside of the McDonald's near Holly Hall. When the manager told about a recent job applicant who complained about the job hours, she replied, "You wouldn't hear me complain!" In a matter of moments she was employed, and a sign went up under the golden arches, "McGranny Works Here." She became quite a celebrity, appearing in news stories and even making a TV commercial.

As McGranny, she greets children, wipes tables, and talks to customers. When she is asked what she does she replies, "I play with the children and talk to good looking men." People come from far and near to visit her, and she often says, "I'm having the time of my life! I'm just a country girl who loves people." Such is Angie McGranny.

 PRAYER

Loving Lord, who cooked breakfast for the disciples and fed the hungry multitudes, thank you for older people who feed the hungry in restaurants, soup kitchens, and other places. Amen.

# 59

Therefore, since we are surrounded by such a great cloud of witnesses, let us throw off everything that hinders and the sin that so easily entangles, and let us run with perseverance the race marked out for us.

Hebrews 12:1

## READ FOR REFLECTION

> So tired! So tired!
> So tired of being pushed around.
> God, give me the strength to fight,
> To fight 'til the sun goes down.
> God, give me strength to fight,
> To fight 'til victory is won.
> O God, I'm so tired! *So tired!*
> So tired of being pushed around.

ESTELLE ATLEY EATON
("So Tired")

## MEDITATION

### *So Tired of Being Pushed Around*

It was a memorable visit. Estelle was 103 years old and still lived alone, surrounded by a room full of memoirs. Her face, lined with the years, beamed as she remembered her roots and her Native American father.

A plaque on the wall honoring Estelle on her 100th birthday as a "World Traveler, Christian Leader, and Poet" caught my eye. She read her poem, "So Tired!" and told me that she could have been Rosa Parks.

One day years ago, when African Americans were forced to sit in the back of buses, Estelle Atley Eaton tried to send her nephew home. The seats in the back of the bus were full; the seats in the front were empty. The driver refused to let Eaton's nephew sit in one of the empty seats because of his skin color, so rather than make the boy stand, Eaton told the driver that they would wait for the next bus. They sat in the bus terminal for three more hours, waiting for the bus. While they waited, she wrote "So Tired of Being Pushed Around."

She told me that experience taught her a lesson. "My whole philosophy changed. From then on, I fought that battle with love, not hate. Young, old, color—they aren't in my vocabulary."

I asked for her philosophy of life. Quietly she replied, "Jesus made it so clear. On his way to the cross, he told us to go out and love people. My favorite words of counsel are, 'Love' and 'Don't give up.'" Being in her presence made me aware we *are* surrounded by so great a cloud of witnesses.

 **PRAYER**

Gracious God, who bears our burdens even when they seem so heavy, give us grace never to give up, and always to love people. Amen.

# 60

. . . with a little boy to lead them.

Isaiah 11:6 (NJB)

## READ FOR REFLECTION

In my country, aged people have the right to live with the younger people. It is the grandparents who tell fairy tales to the children. When they get old, their skin is cold and wrinkled, and it is a great joy for them to hold their grandchild, so warm and tender.

THICH NHAT HANH

## MEDITATION

### *Grace from a Grandchild*

Most of our grandchildren are in distant places, and we only see them on rare visits. So we stay in contact with them through telephone and written notes. We fill albums with endless pictures and are always amazed at how quickly they grow.

Recently, I went with one of my grandsons, Thomas, age three, to a marina to feed the ducks. When he spied the ducks his face lit up, and he exclaimed, "Man, do you see those ducks?" Then for a moment he paused and said, "Wait a minute. I'm not a man, I'm just little Thomas!" It was a moment of grace. I wish all of us could have such a positive self image.

Sometimes I believe one of the greatest sources of wisdom for older people can be found in being a little child again. Jesus said, "Unless you change and become like little children, you will never enter the kingdom of heaven" (Matthew 18:3).

Becoming a child again means a new dependence. For the first twenty years or so of life, we depend on parents and friends. Then we become independent, and the older we become, the more people we again need.

Is it any wonder that the prophet Isaiah says that "a little boy shall lead them"? We learn from our grandchildren the need to be dependent once again, that we are indeed children of God.

 **PRAYER**

Our Parent, once again we are dependent on you as we were when we were children. No matter what happens, we know that you are our stay. Amen.

# 61

He who goes out weeping, carrying seed to sow, will return with songs of joy, carrying sheaves with him.

Psalm 126:6

## READ FOR REFLECTION

It always seemed strange to me that people would speak about the autumn of life, the golden years, as being the best of seasons. It is not so with the trees whose colors are the reason for calling the autumn "golden." For them, their golden hues are a sign of ending, a going towards winter sleep. It is a time for losing past beauty. . . . The trees may look their prettiest in autumn, but in fact, they are losing their moment in the sun. . . .

Humans, of course, are quite different from trees. In their late autumn days of age, they can *remember* and *foresee*. They can remember the flowers of their spring and the vigor of their summer. They can foresee what lies ahead . . . the dead of winter. In their autumn days humans can "feel" old, and that feeling makes the days seem less than perfect. Fearing the future, they are forced to look back to find the truly golden years. . . .

 If we look at the succession of seasons that have flowed through our years, we should know that winter is not the end of everything. It is just a resting period before a new and glorious spring. The message of the seasons and the message of Christianity is that indeed there *are* Golden Years, and they lie just ahead—even though we may now be in the autumn of our life.

DONALD X. BURT

## MEDITATION

### *Autumn Years*

I hadn't seen Philip in years. He had known real tragedy since his retirement. His wife was killed in a senseless automobile wreck, and one of his sons was in prison. He had known enough sorrow to have defeated other men. Yet Philip had not surrendered to despair. He triumphed over his troubles. He had taken a grandson into his home and become his mentor. He was still active as a consultant, offering the harvest of his years, bundled by experience and wisdom. There was a different quality of light on his face, an autumn wisdom.

Psalm 126 reflects the joy of the farmer, who sows his seed with tears and reaps a rich harvest with joy. We sow the seeds of life in the springtime, when life bursts forth in newness and joy. We plow the fields in the warm, summer months, when our relentless energy drives us to ceaseless activity. But the autumn years not only bring slower steps but mingled experiences of sadness and joy.

A touch of autumn in the air is a reminder of the coming of winter. As the psalmist expressed it, "You sweep men away in the sleep of death . . ." (Psalm 90:5). Sadness of farewells are too common in the autumn years. Yet, beyond winter is a more glorious spring . . . a resurrection morning that brings eternal life. The ancient psalmist prayed that God would "restore their fortunes like streams in the Negev." They knew this dry territory to the south of Judah is quickly changed by autumn rains into a place of life-giving streams.

 **PRAYER**

Autumn is my season, Lord. I'll walk through the fallen leaves and think about what's ended in my life . . . and what's beginning now, and in the life to come. Amen.

How precious to me are your thoughts, O God! How vast is the sum of them! . . . When I awake, I am still with you.

Psalm 139:17-18

## READ FOR REFLECTION

I am now
   in my final years . . .
      and your WISDOM
         is ripe in me.

I keep thinking
   I should HARVEST it . . .
      and put it in your storehouse . . .
        but my feet
           begin to falter.

I am slipping
   and staggering
      when I should be
        SPRINTING.

Help me cling
   to a FAITH
      that YOU are
      HERE
        in the weakness of my age.

LLOYD REMINGTON
(from "Dawn to Dusk")

## *Wisdom for Older People*

There is a hidden danger lurking in the latest image of aging: the so called youthful achiever. While it is better than being seen as passive victims, highlighting older persons' youthfulness and praising them for looking young has its dangers. Many older people simply cannot be like Jane Fonda or Joan Collins, or be glamorous models of youth.

That is why Psalm 139 is precious scripture for older people. John Calvin said of the Psalms, "I am in the habit of calling this book . . . 'The Anatomy of all Parts of the Soul,' for not an affection will anyone find in himself, an image of which is not reflected in this mirror."

Psalm 139 makes it clear that God knows us intimately and loves us as we are: "LORD, you have searched me and you know me . . . You are familiar with all my ways." When an older person feels insignificant or known only as someone's grandmother, this psalm says, "You are somebody," because God cares for you. As an older person, there are times when you think no one cares whether you exist or not, when you feel rejected and discarded, but God thinks about you.

This is wisdom . . . to know that whatever happens to us in old age, God's presence goes with us. "Where can I go from your Spirit? Where can I flee from your presence?" The darkness of depression, inevitable losses of later life, death itself, are not off limits to this God!

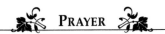 **PRAYER**

Read Psalm 139 again as a prayer. Amen.

# 63

They all joined together constantly in prayer, along with the women and Mary the mother of Jesus . . .

Acts 1:14

## READ FOR REFLECTION

Come, ye elders, those engaging
In the art of growing old;
Let us celebrate our aging,
Let our gratitude be told.

God, we praise thee; Lord, we thank thee,
For thy blessing manifold.

Nature still her bounty showers
For our pleasure every day;
Sunlight, moon-glow, rain and flowers,
Creatures small and children gay.

God, we praise thee; Lord, we thank thee;
Ever gratefully we pray.

Loving friendships long enduring
Sweeten hours with gracious thought.
Others, with their tender caring,
Comfort, peace and joy have brought.

God, we praise thee; Lord, we thank thee;
For thy grace bestowed unsought.

GENEVIEVE LEXOW
("Come, Ye Elders, Those Engaging")

## MEDITATION

### *Mary: Prototype of Elder Wisdom*

We usually think of Mary as the young woman chosen by God to be the mother of Jesus. We think of her early life, the Annunciation, her Magnificat, and her motherly care of the child Jesus. We remember her lonely vigil at the Crucifixion, the intensity of her suffering as she watched her son endure the agony and terror of the cross. The words of old Simeon had come true, "A sword will pierce your own soul too" (Luke 2:35). We watch her leave the cross, saddened and bereaved, as John takes her into his own home.

Yet, Mary is the patroness of the elderly, and one who proclaimed the wonder of God in old age. She becomes a spiritual elder to the young church. Most scholars believe that Dr. Luke received many stories of Jesus' life from Mary when she visited Paul in prison in Caesarea. What Mary had treasured and pondered in her heart became holy scripture.

May we too proclaim the wonder of God and "let our gratitude be told."

 **PRAYER**

God, we praise Thee; Lord, we thank Thee. Fill our hearts with love and joy. Amen.

# 64

READ ACTS 5:33-42

Then one in the council stood up, a Pharisee named Gamaliel, . . . [and he said] keep away from these men and let them alone; for if this plan or this work is of men, it will come to nothing; but if it is of God, you cannot overthrow it—lest you even be found to fight against God.

Acts 5:34, 38-39 (NKJV)

## READ FOR REFLECTION

What can we say about wisdom? Certainly it is one of the qualities most often admired in old people, and in part because they are old. They have been around a long time. They were "not born yesterday." They are seasoned, aged in the wood. They "know the road."

B. F. SKINNER

## *Caution Comes with Age*

Gamaliel was a respected sage of the Sanhedrin. He was said to have been Paul's teacher (Acts 22:3). He showed remarkable caution when the Sanhedrin wanted more extreme measures taken against the young Christian church.

E. P. Blair claims that Gamaliel's caution may have been due to "his characteristically tolerant and generous spirit . . . or to a true piety which divined in the events he had witnessed the purpose and power of God at work." Whatever his motives, he showed remarkable wisdom when the Pharisees were crying for blood.

Balanced judgment, a careful weighing of evidence, a willingness not to act rashly are marks of wisdom. Although wisdom is usually associated with mature years, this is not universally true. The Bible recognizes the tragedy of age without wisdom, and the possibility of wisdom in the young. "Better," declares Koheleth, "is a poor and wise youth than an old and foolish king" (Ecclesiastes 4:13, NKJV). However, as Robert W. Carlson says, "While wisdom does not come automatically with old age, wisdom seldom comes without the honing of life that long experience brings."

Gamaliel's wisdom proved prophetic. If the Pharisees had taken more extreme measures against the Christians, they would have been fighting God. History later proved God's vindication of the disciples.

Let us learn from our elders and not be impulsive or quick to condemn; but with a cautious compassion, let God be the judge.

 PRAYER

When we are tempted to rush into things without thinking, help us, O God, to remember the wisdom of Gamaliel. Amen.

# 65

I thank my God upon every remembrance of you, always in every prayer of mine making request for you all with joy . . .

Philippians 1:3-4 (NKJV)

## READ FOR REFLECTION

Last year I visited my grandfather, C. Rees Jenkins, at the infirmary of Sharon Towers, a Presbyterian retirement home in Charlotte, North Carolina. I arrived just as my aunt was reading scripture very loudly into his hearing aid. I waited outside. Grandfather was ninety-four at the time, a retired Presbyterian minister. . . .

"Amen," I heard my aunt and my grandfather say together, and her chair slid a bit as she got up to leave. He said something to her that I could not make out, but everyone on the hall could hear her shouted reply, "All we need is for you to keep praying! Just keep praying. Nothing is more important than that!" . . .

Finally we prayed together. . . . And for a moment, it occurred to me that I was the beneficiary of countless more prayers prayed in this place. It occurred to me that God may be less lonely in this place filled with prayers than in most of creation. . . . In the end all we need is for those in places filled with prayers to keep praying until time or calling brings us to inhabit those places, to search and find. And be found. Nothing is more important.

MARSHALL JENKINS

## MEDITATION

### *Just Keep Praying!*
### *Nothing Is More Important Than That*

Marshall Jenkin's touching story of his ninety-four-year old grandfather's prayers cuts to the heart of spiritual wisdom. A man who had been "a blur of perpetual motion" found himself unable to do the ministry which had been his life. But, he was reminded, "Keep on praying," for as James reminds us, "The effective, fervent prayer of a righteous man avails much" (James 5:16, NKJV).

Prayer is such a vital ministry. Paul was confined to a Roman jail, yet he wrote the Philippians that he remembered them constantly in prayer. Separated by distance, confined by a prison cell, Paul's ministry continued through fervent, effective prayer. Many older persons also use periods of inactivity to make more of their prayer life. These silent pray-ers touch the lives of many. The words of James Montgomery sum it well:

> Prayer is the Christian's vital breath,
> The Christian's native air,
> [The] watchword at the gates of death;
> He [or she] enters heaven with prayer.

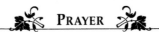 **PRAYER**

Lord, teach us not only how to pray when we are older, but that our prayers do matter. Amen.

Then Samson prayed to the LORD, "O Sovereign LORD, remember me. O God, please strengthen me just once more . . ."

Judges 16:28

## READ FOR REFLECTION

He moved on down the path to a stone wall. Why this wall was there was a mystery, since it enclosed no space and marked no boundary. . . .

There were two ways to deal with this wall if he wanted to go farther. The most serious possibility was to do what Samson did when he asked God for one more shot at the Philistines. . . . One route around the wall is to return to the fray, mover and shaker. Show 'em what he can do. He knew it was foolish. Plain dumb. But he might do it.

The other possibility was to accept the implications of his own preaching of the gospel. Let it go. To let some things go, at least. Freedom is rooted in part in the trust that God will take the things of our hands and weave them into a future more gracious than the present. . . .

Whatever the original reason for its being there, he knew that this wall now served to require a decision of him; which way around, or perhaps, over. Though he had little hair left, he could still take hold of the pillars. Or he could test freedom and trust God.

He stood at the wall for a long time.

JOHN W. VANNORSDALL

## MEDITATION

### *One More Shot or Let It Go?*

It seems to be that older persons are forever faced with the decision to "give it one more shot" or "let it go." Samson asked God for one more shot at the Philistines. He shook the building until it fell, killing more Philistines when he died than he had while he lived. And, Samson is remembered.

Is it wisdom to ask God for strength for "one more shot" when, like Samson, we have little hair left in old age? We shudder at the injustices and lovelessness in the world, and yet we are painfully aware of our limitations. Should we ask God for "one more shot"?

Or is it wisdom to "let it go"? To realize that we have done the best we could, and now it is finally time to practice what we have preached, and let God take control? It is time to believe what the psalmist wrote: "Commit your way to the LORD; trust in him and he will do this" (Psalm 37:5).

It is not an easy decision, whether still to take hold of the pillars or test freedom and trust God. Maybe old age is a time for both. Or maybe a time does finally come when we listen to the wisdom of Jesus: "For whoever wants to save his life will lose it, but whoever loses his life for me and for the gospel will save it" (Mark 8:35).

 PRAYER

God, grant us the courage for one last shot, the serenity of letting it all go, and wisdom to know which is better. Amen.

# 67

Strengthen the feeble hands, steady the knees that give way.

Isaiah 35:3

## READ FOR REFLECTION

What a fellowship, what a joy divine,
Leaning on the everlasting arms;
What a blessedness, what a peace is mine,
Leaning on the everlasting arms.
Leaning, leaning, Safe and secure from all alarms;
Leaning, leaning, Leaning on the everlasting arms.

ELISHA A. HOFFMAN

## *Braced for Success*

For some time I have suffered from osteoarthritis in my hands, a nagging problem for a writer. I finally gave up and went to a rheumatologist, who providentially put me in touch with seventy-three-year-old Lurleen Collum of Odessa, Texas, who has invented the Collum Thumb Brace.

It all began with her own needs. She, also, had severe arthritis in her hands, and since she had made leg weights following surgery to her kneecap, she was encouraged to make thumb braces and sell them at a reasonable price. Armed with scrap leather, a sewing machine, and tenacity, Lurleen designed a thumb brace. She now operates out of her home and makes Collum Thumb Braces.

She has survived many difficult moments in her life, including the death of her husband and the death of her only child. A hard and diligent worker, Lurleen has driven a truck at an army air base, has done wartime factory work, and has engaged in other business ventures.

For the last eight years she has marketed this helpful brace for arthritis sufferers. I owe her a debt of gratitude because her creativity has braced my hands for more writing and driving. Lurleen Collum is a classic example of an older person who used her ingenuity to design a helpful service for older persons. She has literally "strengthened the feeble hands" of many older people. In so doing she has helped more people than even she knows.

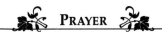 PRAYER

When we are tempted to give up, or resign ourselves to being useless, help us, like Lurleen, to design new ways to help others. Amen.

## 68

Is not wisdom found among the aged? Does not long life bring understanding?

Job 12:12

## READ FOR REFLECTION

From the moment of our conception life is graced by God, and he does not limit his gifts to our active years. Looking back we can see how times of difficulty were actually the rich garnering periods. The years of diminishment can also bring moments in which God is closer than he ever was in our busy, time-clock pressured years. . . .

MARY HESTER VALENTINE

## MEDITATION

### *I've Enjoyed Every Minute of It*

"I've enjoyed every minute of it." These were not the words of a talented musician reveling in a glorious performance or of a youthful athlete basking in her moment of glory at the Olympics. They were spoken by Miss Mary McCorkle, a 104-year-old lady who used those words to summarize her life.

She did not deny the ravages of old age. "I can't see, I can't hear, I can't walk, and my hair is falling out," she said, "But every day I live the world is more beautiful. I can still read my large-print Bible, watch the changing seasons from my window, and do some baking and canning from my wheelchair."

Mary McCorkle was the first home health nurse in Lincoln County, North Carolina, and her real love was the children. Her eyes twinkled as she recalled their names . . . and their antics. I asked her what she would say to my grandchildren and she replied, "Go to school. Do what is right with all your might, and God will take care of you."

Such a charming, winsome lady, still staying in touch with life and enjoying every day. Mary invited me to have a piece of cake she had baked, and then we said our good-byes. I left remembering Erik Erikson's words that old age either means despair or integrity. This lady epitomized integrity, a life lived well, and every minute enjoyed.

 PRAYER

Ancient of Days, if you allow us to live a long life, may we have the spirit and attitude of Mary McCorkle. Amen.

# VII

# The Final Wisdom: Learning From Death

*If there is no meaning in older age, wouldn't it be better if we could die at a chosen time so that we are not a burden for society and for ourselves? Is there meaning in life for an older person, and can old age be meaningful for those around the elderly? These are the fundamental questions that will influence not only our way of life but also our retirement and our own death and dying process.*

*Leo E. Missinne*

# 69

But God said to him, "You fool! This night your soul will be required of you; then whose will those things be which you have provided?"

Luke 12:20 (NKJV)

## READ FOR REFLECTION

In facing death as a transition to another life, or as the end of a journey, many dying older adults like to repair what can be repaired and make peace with themselves and others. They want to talk about all the important things in their life, and they must be allowed to do it.

LEO E. MISSINNE

## MEDITATION

### *Are Your Bags Packed for Eternity?*

The tragedy of the rich farmer in Jesus' parable was not that he had acquired wealth dishonestly or was punished by a sudden death, but that he had not prepared for death. Just when he decided to pull down his barns, expand his assets, and retire to a life of leisure, death knocked at his door.

Facing the inevitability of death is not a morbid preoccupation, but a realistic and spiritual task. Only after we have prepared for death, can we truly live. It is liberating to settle those matters, and then go on with life.

My friend was a simple old man. Most of his life was lived quietly in the community, working in the shops, serving in the church, loving his family. When he died, his widow shared with me that he had prepared for his death in every detail. Not only in arrangements for his funeral and burial, but in talking with his family, and sharing some last wishes before he died. Unlike the rich farmer, this poor worker was ready.

At his funeral I read a prayer by W.E.B. Du Bois which seemed to summarize his life. Let us pray Du Bois's prayer today.

 PRAYER

We thank Thee, O Lord, for the gift of Death—for the great silence that follows the jarring noises of the world—the rest that is Peace. We who live to see the passing of that fine and simple Old Man, who has so often sat beside us here in this room, must not forget the legacy he leaves us or the Hope he still holds to us. Amen.

W.E.B. Du Bois

## 70

And as it is appointed for men to die once, but after this the judgment, so Christ was offered once to bear the sins of many.

Hebrews 9:27-28 (NKJV)

## READ FOR REFLECTION

I come back from the cemetery riding up front
in the hearse, back now empty of the casket. . . .

There comes a day when everyone comes back
from the cemetery except me.
I wonder what will happen then.
. . . . . . . . . . . . . . . . . . . . . . . . . . . . . . .
As for my work, if I die tonight, there will be
Church next Sunday, and all of that is as it
ought to be, others going on with the work which
I have done, doing it as well or better.

I am left thus with this lesson, that any
difference my life makes must be the difference
it makes to me and not to others.
Now, let me see, what difference do I want my
life to make for me before that day which is to
be when everybody comes back from the cemetery
except me?

JOHN D. BURTON
(from "When Everybody Comes Back from the Cemetery Except Me")

## MEDITATION

### *When Everybody Comes Back from the Cemetery Except Me*

It is a cold, blustery day at the cemetery. The tent poles over the grave are clanging in the wind. The family is hushed and still. The scriptures are read. Words are spoken. Huddled together for warmth, the people of God say what they believe. I stand, staring at the casket, facing the yawning chasm of unknown worlds, grieving the loss of a friend, and think of John Burton's poem.

There will come a day when "everybody will come back from the cemetery except me." It will be my turn. The curtain of life will fall, the crowd will file out, and the theater will be dark. Death becomes so much closer as you grow older and your friends leave and you cling to what is left.

An elderly gentleman whom I visited once told me, "I play a game when I read the obituaries. If the people who died are older than I, I win; if they are younger, I lose." The day comes when we begin losing . . . and realize that our rendezvous with death is not far away.

What has my life meant? What difference has my life made? Have I really mattered to anyone? These are my questions on that day when I remember John Burton's poem.

 PRAYER

Great Merciful God, when this life is over and everyone returns from the cemetery except me, your steadfast love awaits me. Amen.

# 71

Jesus replied, "The hour has come for the Son of Man to be glorified. I tell you the truth, unless a kernel of wheat falls to the ground and dies, it remains only a single seed. But if it dies, it produces many seeds."

John 12:23-24

## READ FOR REFLECTION

Ruth had ovarian cancer. Her "kernel of wheat" was falling to the ground to die. Her body was "wasting away." As a pastor, I have watched many "kernels" fall to the ground.

Bedridden, jaundiced, and heavily medicated, Ruth was in the final stage. The weekend had been rough. On Monday morning I stopped by for a visit. She was awake and able to talk.

I remember saying to her, "Ruth, your body is worn out. It can't carry you much farther. But the Ruth inside—the warm, humorist Ruth who loves to travel and be with her friends—she is very much alive. She will not die."

I said a prayer and asked for God's angels of mercy to come and help Ruth make her journey. I closed with the Lord's Prayer. Ruth couldn't say it with me, but when I finished she said a big "Amen!"

That was at 10:00 A.M. At 2:00 P.M. that afternoon, the "kernel of wheat" fell to the ground and died. Jesus says this has to happen and in the process, "it produces many seeds." Amen!

STEVEN P. EASON

## MEDITATION

### *Coming to Terms with Death*

Some people teach us how to live. Esther taught us how to die. At an early age she heard the dreaded news that her cancer was inoperable and her days numbered. Yet it seemed as if she had come to terms with death before this ever happened. She met death bravely and without flinching.

In her last days at home, blessed by the tender care of Hospice, she amazed everyone at how she met death with such candor . . . as if it were but another chapter in her life story. She spoke openly about her death, said her good-byes, and even joked about it. On a day everyone expected her to die, she lived out the day, and told us, "Well, I guess I surprised everyone by not dying today."

Several years later her husband died from cancer. He also faced his end with raw courage and resolute faith in God. A week before he was buried beside his wife, he had me write down what he wanted said at his funeral. "Not only did Esther teach people to die. She taught *me* how to die."

Esther reminded me of Queen Esther who went before the king at the risk of her life, and whose courage saved her people from destruction. She came to that awesome moment of death with courage and faith. A witness to us all.

 **PRAYER**

Lord, you have given me this brief life; may I receive it with grace, and live each day with joy. Help me to prepare for death, assured you will be with me at that moment when I step out into the final darkness. Amen.

They went to a place called Gethsemane, and Jesus said to his disciples, "Sit here while I pray." . . . and he began to be deeply distressed and troubled. "My soul is overwhelmed with sorrow to the point of death . . ."

Mark 14:32-34

## READ FOR REFLECTION

Our relationship has been that of a fencing duel. I, fighting with all my heart, all my energy, and with the resources of my mind. You fought lightheartedly—even teasingly—because you knew in the end that only you could be the victor.

> The usual feints
> I won, you won
> I discovered a new weapon—interest
> I found I could be cold and unemotional
>     about you
> And so defeat you
> You found John and so defeated me
> And realized my love, teased and tortured him
>     until he died
> Times that I thought I would win
> Times that I wished you would
> But now the battle's over
> Relief
> The peace of not having to fight ever again
> Perhaps I will forget what it is to "be strong"
> You see, I knew all along.

LAURA BOONE
("Death Is But a Horizon")

## *Death Is Ever with Us*

Twenty years ago Laura Boone, a young college student, wrote this poem about death. She had cancer, and while in a cancer ward in a hospital she became engaged to a man with cancer. Six months later her fiancee died. She, however, survived cancer, and now is serving as a nurse and is the mother of two little girls.

The insight about death in her poem is still valid. As a young person she realized the reality of death and felt the agonizing struggle when death knocks at one's door.

Contrast young Laura's insight about death with that of ninety-year-old Lottie. Now confined to her home, she spends most of her time on her couch near the window where she awaits visits from her friends. On one occasion Lottie requested that I read a stanza from a poem by William Cullen Bryant at her funeral. A few lines of that stanza read:

> By an unfaltering trust, approach thy grave
> Like one who wraps the drapery of his couch
> About him and lies down to pleasant dreams.

Like Laura and Lottie, we need to affirm our own death, even as Jesus did in the Garden of Gethsemane. Only then can we live our final years with dignity and grace.

 **PRAYER**

God of grace, help us to realize that the tragedy of life is not in death, but in what dies within us as we live—the death of hope, the death of awareness of the pain of others, the death of faith that love never loses its own. Amen.

Then Israel said to Joseph, "I did not think I should ever see you again, and now God has let me see your children as well! . . . Then Israel said to Joseph, "Now I am about to die. But God will be with you and take you back to the land of your ancestors."

Genesis 48:11, 21 (NJB)

## READ FOR REFLECTION

In giving programs about hospice care, some of the angriest people I have encountered were those who were not able to make a final farewell. They felt cheated out of the opportunity to say good-bye; were not able to say how much they loved this person.

THOMAS A. WELK

## MEDITATION

### *When It Is Time to Say Good-bye*

Picture the moment from holy history. Jacob is fully aware that his death is imminent. Yet life has ended with unbelievable joy since he has been reunited with his lost son, Joseph. . . . So now he blesses Manasseh and Ephraim and, with emotions beyond description, says good-bye. The scriptures tell us that a few days later, "When Jacob had finished giving instructions to his sons, he drew his feet up into the bed, breathed his last and was gathered to his people" (Gen. 49:33).

It is never easy to say good-bye, and the last good-byes are the hardest. When a friend died, we gathered at his death bed and felt that silence beyond words when death is near. He gave permission to say, "Good-bye," and we hugged, grasped his hand, and said our good-byes as his spirit left this world. We thanked him for what he had meant to us and reassured him of God's presence into the next world. He smiled and was gone.

Yet, some of the pain of his loss was eased by our good-byes. Joyce Rupp reminds us that "good-bye was a blessing of love, proclaiming the belief that if God went with you, you would never be alone."* We felt that peaceful blessing at our friend's death bed that day. It was like saying good-bye to a friend we would see again sometime.

 **PRAYER**

Source of life, give us strength when it is time to say goodbye and assurance that we are not alone. Amen.

---

*A beautiful ritual of saying farewell to one who is leaving can be found in Joyce Rupp's book, Praying Our Good-byes, pp. 132–134.

O death, your sentence is welcome to one in want, whose strength is failing, to one worn out with age and a thousand worries, resentful and impatient!

Ecclesiasticus 41:2 (NJB)

## READ FOR REFLECTION

Because we believe all life is a sacred gift from God, something in us wants to prosecute those who help someone die. But after hearing the whole story, juries can rarely be persuaded to convict. Their caution seems to reflect a growing consensus that what is being done by the Kevorkians, the Gilberts, and the Linareses in our country is deeply tragic, but perhaps not wholly wrong.

GERALD OOSTERVEEN

---

\*Ecclesiasticus is found in the Apocrypha in Protestant translations of the Bible.

## *Prolonging Life or Pulling the Plug?*

A friend has had three major brain surgeries, and for months has been in a coma. The family keeps constant vigil, uncertain whether to take "heroic measures" to preserve his life, or to "pull the plug." Since he has not signed a Living Will, they have no choice but to allow life supports. The surgeon seems hesitant to discuss the situation, yet the chaplain feels the family is being deceived by a conspiracy of silence.

When I visit Steve, he makes no response, but once he grasped my hand. I agonize for the family as they hold a harrowing death watch and wonder what is the loving thing to do.

When situations like these arise, especially with the frail elderly, do we love our loved ones enough to let them go? Is life a gift of God, and if so, can only God take it away? Is it morally acceptable for a person to terminate his or her own life? As our life span is extended by medical technology, we will be increasingly confronted with some hard questions. We may have prolonged life, but have we emptied it of its substance?

Koheleth advises, ". . . do not be a fool—why die before your time? . . . The man who fears God will avoid all extremes" (Eccles. 7:17, 18). Yet a peaceful death with dignity, is every person's wish. Every death is different from any that has gone before it. But today we *can* make some hard decisions about our death, thus relieving our families of that burden if such decisions need to be made later. It is a personal decision.

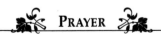 **PRAYER**

Gracious God, help us to commit our spirits to you every day and so end our days in your presence. Amen.

Now we know that if this earthly tent we live in is destroyed, we have a building from God, an eternal house in heaven, not built by human hands.

2 Corinthians 5:1

## READ FOR REFLECTION

We know, of course, that the end of old age, the last end, is death. We cannot hide this from ourselves, even if we are so passionately attached to life that all thought of death is far from our minds, and even if the death of others is not enough to make us think of our own. It is no good behaving like an ostrich! . . .

Old age is the anteroom in which we wait for death. We may have to sit there for a short time or for a long time, as we do in the doctor's waiting room. But we can be quite sure that sooner or later death will open the door and beckon us. Whether we are ready or not, we shall have to respond to that call. . . .

The Christian cannot think of death as a final shipwreck, the breaking up of all life. It is quite the opposite. It is a fulfillment, bringing with it the fullness of maturity. . . . Death sums up our life and gives it its full meaning. . . .

We must never be afraid of death, but look forward to it as the fulfillment of a hope. When the door of the anteroom opens, we shall not see the old man with a scythe and an hourglass emerge, but our good and lovely sister, dressed in white and crowned with a garland of flowers.

JOSEPH FOLLIET

## MEDITATION

### *Settling into Heaven*

Miss Olive and Miss Martha had been Baptist missionaries in China and close friends for years. When old age crept up on them, Miss Olive went to a nursing home. Miss Martha died, and when friends went to tell Miss Olive that her lifelong friend had died, she bowed her head, folded her hands, and prayed: "Dear Jesus, please help Martha get settled in."

It seems to me there is something profound about death in that simple prayer. Jesus told us that he had gone to prepare a place for us. Paul reassured us that when this body we live in is destroyed, God has prepared a new home for us in heaven. So our prayer is that some day we, too, will get settled in.

I remember a story from years ago (source unknown) of a little boy dying with leukemia. One night his mother read the story of King Arthur and the knights of the round table, and how many of them died fighting for the cause. Suddenly the little boy asked his mother, "Mommy, what does it mean to die?" She ran to the kitchen for a moment, desperately trying to find the words, and then returned to tell him, "Son, do you remember when you were a very little boy and we took a long trip, and you would fall asleep in the car?"

"Oh, yes," he replied, "And when I woke up the next morning I was in my own bed because Daddy carried me there." "Well, Son, that is what death is. We fall asleep and wake up in the morning in God's house, where we belong, because a loving Father carried us there.

 PRAYER

Loving God, help us to have that childlike faith about death—that we get settled in your home when we die. Amen.

# 76

Suddenly an angel of the Lord appeared and a light shone in the cell. He tapped Peter on the side and woke him, saying, "Get up quickly." And the chains fell off his wrists.

Acts 12:7 (NRSV)

## READ FOR REFLECTION

> Under the wide and starry sky,
> Dig the grave and let me lie.
> Glad did I live and gladly die,
> And I laid me down with a will.
>
> This be the verse you grave for me:
> *Here he lies where he longed to be;*
> *Home is the sailor, home from sea,*
> *And the hunter home from the hill.*

ROBERT LOUIS STEVENSON
("Requiem")

## Meditation

### *Where No Chains Can Bind Me*

In a famous book of anatomy used in the Middle Ages are the words *MORS ULTIMA LINEA RERUM—Death the Last Line of Things*. Death writes the last line of every person's life, and there is an awesome finality about that.

Yet, there is something liberating about death, despite its finality. Peter was imprisoned by Herod, bound with two chains. But an angel of the Lord appeared, told Peter to "get up quickly," and his chains fell off as he walked into freedom. It seems to me that death liberates us from the chains of this life as we walk into the blinding light of eternity.

The Negro slaves had keen insight into the meaning of death and the hope of a better world beyond. Their slavery on this earth would be vindicated by an incredible freedom over Jordan. This belief was poignantly expressed in this spiritual:

> Deep, deep river,
> my home is over Jordan—
> Deep, deep river, Lord,
> I want to cross over into campground.
> O don't you want to go
> to that gospel feast,
> That promis'd land
> where all is peace?

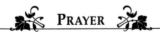 PRAYER

Lord God, let us remember the liberty that death brings:
Free at last! Free at last!
Thank God A'mighty. I'm free at last! Amen.

# 77

Lord, now You are letting Your servant depart in peace . . .

Luke 2:29 (NKJV)

## READ FOR REFLECTION

"Peace" is a great word. Peace is what you feel after a good friend and you have an argument and clear the air. Peace is what you feel after you apologize and it is accepted. Peace is what you feel on Christmas morning. Peace is what you feel when you finally get a letter from someone who was lost but now is found. Peace is Sunday night, at home with your family. Peace is the third day of a two-week vacation. Peace is coffee on the deck with the kids all in bed. Peace is sitting together quietly, or hearing the doctor say, "Everything went fine. He's going to be O.K.!" That's peace.

Death is also peace. Hard for us to imagine, but according to Jesus, it's true. Real peace, permanent peace, eternal peace is waiting for us at the end of this life.

*Lord, now You are letting Your servant depart in peace . . .*

STEVEN P. EASON

## MEDITATION

### *Lord, Let Me Depart in Peace*

Death stood at the door. This dear old man hovered in the valley of the shadow. I had been called to his bedside by the family to be present for his final hours. His sister-in-law, who had kept a constant vigil of love, told me he had made a death wish some months ago. "As I get near the end," he had said, "I have my doubts about many things in life. But I hope I can leave this earth with dignity . . . my faith in God is stronger than ever."

She showed me a picture of him from earlier years. He seemed so vibrant and full of life then, and now so forlorn and hopeless, gasping for that final breath. Then he was gone. I held his hand until his hold ended, almost symbolic of giving up and letting go. But he died in dignity. No respirator kept him from his date with destiny or his meeting with the God he loved. There was the sadness of farewell, but also gratitude that his wish had been granted.

We all proceed every day to our final destiny. If we are wise, we will accept its finality with gratitude; if we are sensible we prepare for it now. If we are blessed, we will depart, as Simeon prayed, in peace . . . and dignity.

 **PRAYER**

Lord, when you call us to leave this world for a better world, may we depart in peace . . . and dignity. Amen.

# 78

A voice is heard in Ramah, weeping and great mourning, Rachel weeping for her children and refusing to be comforted, because they are no more.

Matthew 2:18

## READ FOR REFLECTION

May 12, 1991

Mother, if I had known how you wept
in closets, I would have come;
but you wept quietly for forty years
and died, hardly remembering your name.
We die the death we deserve, some say;
but you never deserved Parkinson's—
or sitting in the corner chair alone.

. . . . . . . . . . . . . . . . . . . . . . . . . . . . . . . . .

Mother, I try to remember for you,
hoping that in shared memories you join me still. . . .

JOHN C. MORGAN
(from "If I Had Known, Mother")

## *Untimely Death*

The slaughter of the innocent children in Bethlehem and its vicinity at the birth of Jesus is seen by Matthew as a fulfillment of Jeremiah's prophecy that Rachel would weep for her children. Yet, it was Rachel who died an untimely death in childbirth.

John Morgan's poem shows in poignant words how sad and tragic was the untimely death of our mother. She who had to nurse two sons through life-threatening illnesses that brought us to the gates of death, died herself at an early age.

Some do experience an untimely death, robbed of the longer years we enjoy. While others, like Sarah and Elizabeth Delany, not only encounter longevity but also are able to tell their incredible life story to the masses. In their book, *Having Our Say*, Sarah speaks of death and dying: "Over the years, we've buried a lot of people. Even the generation younger than us is starting to die off. I don't know why I am still here and they're not, but I don't fret over it. It is in God's hands. . . . I don't worry about dying, and neither does Bessie. We are at peace. You do kind of wonder, when's it going to happen? That's why you learn to love each and every day, child."

What a beautiful attitude toward death. Sarah's comforting words are an adaptation of Romans 14:8: "If we live, we live to the Lord; and if we die, we die to the Lord. So, whether we live or die, we belong to the Lord."

 PRAYER

Father of love, we realize that in life as well as in death, we belong to you. Amen.

# 79

For I am already being poured out like a drink offering, and the time has come for my departure. I have fought the good fight, I have finished the race, I have kept the faith.

2 Timothy 4:6-7

## READ FOR REFLECTION

We too take ship, O soul
Joyous we too launch out on trackless seas . . .
Caroling free, singing our song of God,
Chanting our chant of pleasant exploration . . .
Sail forth—steer for the deep waters only,
Reckless, O soul, exploring, I with thee, and thou
    with me,
For we are bound where the mariner has not yet dared
    to go,
And we will risk the ship, ourselves and all.

O my brave soul!
O farther, farther sail!
O daring joy but safe! are they not all the seas of God?
O farther, farther, farther, sail.

WALT WHITMAN
(from "The Song of the Open Road")

## MEDITATION

### *Departure to a Greater Destiny*

In some of his final words to Timothy, Paul talks about his death, that the time has come for his departure. The word *departure* is a nautical term; it suggests a ship which has been moored to the shore, the rope flung off, the anchor lifted, and the ship moving out of harbor into the wide and boundless sea.

Paul sees death as a moment for new adventure, not a time for defeat or sadness. It is not like an old half-ruined wreck of a ship putting into port; rather, it is a ship which has cast off the ropes which bind us to this world to sail into unknown waters where God becomes present. Only on the sea can the ship fulfill the possibility of its own being, and fulfill the purpose for which it was made.

The apostle John made this clear when he wrote, "Beloved, we are God's children now; what we will be has not yet been revealed. What we do know is this: when he is revealed, we will be like him, for we will see him as he is" (1 John 3:2, NRSV).

What a blessed departure! May John's words give us strength to fight the good fight, and persistence to keep the faith.

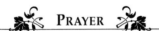 **PRAYER**

"Deep calls unto deep . . ." Lord, when you call us to depart this world, and sail into unknown waters, help us to know your presence and the joy set before us. Amen.

## 80

Precious in the sight of the LORD is the death of his saints.

Psalm 116:15

## READ FOR REFLECTION

Death be not proud, though some have called thee
Mighty and dreadful, for, thou art not so,
For, those, whom thou thinkst, thou dost overthrow,
Die not, poor death, nor yet canst thou kill me.

. . . . . . . . . . . . . . . . . . . . . . . . . . . . . . . . . . . . . . . . . . .

Our short sleep past, we wake eternally,
And death shall be no more; death, thou shalt die.

JOHN DONNE
(from "Holy Sonnets")

---

[*]*Wisdom of Solomon is found in the Apocrypha in Protestant translations of the Bible.*

## MEDITATION

### *Like Enoch She Walked Home*

Miss Etta lived a quiet, unobtrusive life, working diligently at the courthouse and in her yard. Not many people really knew who she was. Except for two occasions, she never traveled more than a hundred miles from her home. Once she suffered a bad accident and had to be moved to a distant hospital. She seemed more intrigued at watching the scenery than complaining about her pain.

She had been the faithful treasurer of her church for over sixty years, and no one knew how many hours she had spent in counting the offering, keeping the books, and protecting her church's money. She never missed a Sunday at church until the ravages of old age struck her. First Parkinson's disease, then cancer stalked her path. Through it all she kept her resolute, quiet faith in God.

She spent her last lonely days in a nursing home. When she realized she would never go home again, she seemed to "give up the ghost." So many of her friends had preceded her in death that only a few gathered for her final rites. Yet that is what she would have wanted—no pomp or circumstance, but a quiet dignity surrounding her departure. Like Enoch, she walked with God, and then was no more because God took her away. She made death so terribly real, a journey home.

 **PRAYER**

Father, help us to do what is right, to love kindness, and to walk humbly with you. Amen.

# 81

Finally, be strong in the Lord and in his mighty power.

Ephesians 6:10

## READ FOR REFLECTION

And when grim Death doth take me by the throat,
Thou wilt have pity on thy handiwork;
Thou wilt not let him on my suffering gloat,
But draw my soul out—gladder than man or boy,
When thy saved creatures from the narrow ark
Rushed out, and leaped and laughed and cried for joy,
And the great rainbow strode across the dark.

GEORGE MACDONALD

## MEDITATION

### *Finally*

Several times in his letters to the young churches Paul uses the word *finally* (2 Cor. 13:11, Phil. 3:1, 4:8; 2 Thess. 3:1). He urged his readers to rejoice and think good thoughts, and requested their prayers. His final word to the Ephesians was: "Finally, be strong in the Lord and in his mighty power."

Death forever remains a mystery. The gates guard their secrets well and few stray beams of light escape through the crevices. But we can be sure that Christ has destroyed death and "brought life and immortality to light through the gospel" (2 Tim. 1:10). That *is* enough.

In some of the final words he wrote before his death, Joseph Sittler says, "The Christian faith says that nothing in human experience is outside the experiences of God . . . The point is that life, which comes from God, is cared for by God and somehow goes back into the life of God."

With Paul, we can affirm, "If we live, we live to the Lord, and if we die, we die to the Lord; so then, whether we live or whether we die, we are the Lord's" (Rom. 14:8, NRSV). What life beyond death might be, I have no notion. Whatever it may be, I am content to leave it in the hands of God . . . there is still time to move on to something important, today.

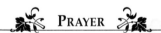 PRAYER

Lord, teach us to live each day as if it were our last. Amen.

P, 93 - Paragraph 3